AF898559

A note to your future self.

Write one word to summarise what you hope these pages will bring you:

BIS Publishers
Timorplein 46
1094 CC Amsterdam
The Netherlands
bis@bispublishers.com
www.bispublishers.com

ISBN 978 90 636 9867 6

Copyright © 2025 Emmi Salonen and BIS Publishers.
2nd printing 2026

Author and designer: Emmi Salonen / Studio Emmi
www.emmi.co.uk

Book website:
www.creativeecosystem.org

Editor: Becca Warner

All rights reserved. No part of this publication may be reproduced or transmitted in any form or by any means, electronic or mechanical, including photocopy, recording or any information storage and retrieval system, without permission in writing from the copyright owners. Every reasonable attempt has been made to identify owners of copyright. Any errors or omissions brought to the publisher's attention will be corrected in subsequent editions.

The Creative Wellbeing Handbook

How to fuel creativity, find balance
and stay inspired

Emmi Salonen

BIS Publishers

Hello, I'm Emmi

I'm a designer, a nature lover and a traveller. I love stationery, plants and spotting how the sky blue of my jumper perfectly complements my morning coffee mug. I'm at my happiest when I'm playing around with things I gather in the forest and losing myself in dance. I can spend hours chatting about life with someone I've just met, or staring at the light falling through a sunlit tree.

Like all of us, I am many things. But there was a point in my life when I lost touch with a lot of who I was, and what brought me joy. I was burned out.

Since starting university, I hadn't stopped. I graduated with my Graphic Design BA from University of Brighton in the UK, then moved to Italy to work at Benetton's Communication Research Centre, Fabrica. From there, I moved to London, then New York, to work at design studios with some of the world's biggest brands as their clients.

Before long, I set up my own design practice, Studio Emmi. It was a move that was as daunting as it was exciting, those early days a heady mix of self-doubt and determination. I put the word out to friends, colleagues, anyone who'd listen – and the first projects began to roll in. I went on to work with clients that included the British Council, the BBC and the Finnish National Gallery, and delivered design work that really meant something to me. I even had the opportunity to lead a creative team at a sustainability agency, where our work reached global audiences and helped shift companies' behaviour for the better.

1

2

3

4

1 Domestika Elm Arts Centre visual identity

2 Hidden Gallery, Alex Financial Services, MO Piano Technician Logo designs

3 The Return of the Gods: Neoclassical Sculpture in Britain Tate Britain exhibition graphics

4 Hidden Gallery Visual identity

From the outside, my career had all the hallmarks of success. I was channelling my creativity into work that mattered, and getting the opportunity to work on a constant stream of varied, intellectually stimulating projects. But I started noticing a new level of exhaustion after work each day. I stopped seeing my friends and started neglecting exercise. Over weeks that became months, I realised I felt increasingly unwell. More worryingly to me, I realised that I no longer wanted to create. The spark was gone – the thrill of new ideas felt like a distant memory.

Frightened, I thought: If I'm no longer a creative, who am I?

Answering this question took me all over the world – and, eventually, right back to my design studio. Happily, creativity is a flame that can be diminished, but not extinguished.

How did my light get so low? Why do others – a worrying 70% of creatives – suffer the same dimming of their spark?[1] And how can they get it back?

1

2

3

4

HARTSWOOD

5

6

1 Pick Me Up at Somerset House Visual identity and exhibition graphics with Chrissie Macdonald, photo by Jess Bonham

2 Artek Product catalogues

3 Local Food Plan Visual identity

4 European Forest Institute Visual identity

5 Hartswood, Greenwood Place, Wonderwater Logo designs

6 Finnish Institute Visual identity

Finding balance

The answers began revealing themselves to me on a long solo trip that I took to connect with and learn from creative people in different places, from different cultures. My journey across continents took me to unfamiliar landscapes – to the volcanic Marquesas Islands in French Polynesia, where it takes only a small leap of imagination to see dinosaurs roaming; on a pilgrimage to Shashamane in Ethiopia; to the striking Pink Sea of Colombia; and to Norway's turquoise Arctic waters.

One hot day, I cycled to the edge of Fakarava, a Polynesian atoll where the ground is made of dead white coral but life below the water is fluorescent, lush, magical. I couldn't be further from my London home, the safe familiarity of the friends and cafes and grey streets that I know. I sat down, and I listened. First the wind told me its business, then the slow waves lapped their thoughts. The sky was quiet and the flora still.

Then, I heard a question I hadn't asked of myself before: How are you?
My reply: I'm not ok.
Why is that?
My answer: I have not given myself what I need to keep going.

It was a simple opening to a conversation that continues to this day. What it revealed to me was profound – that I had lost touch with what I needed, and forgotten to give it to myself.

INSPIRATION EXPEDITION FIELD NOTES
Texture and colour research

This page: Ethiopian dwellings

Right hand page, top: Fakarava coral, French Polynesia
Middle: Algarve shells, Portugal
Bottom: Arctic Circle sketches, Norway

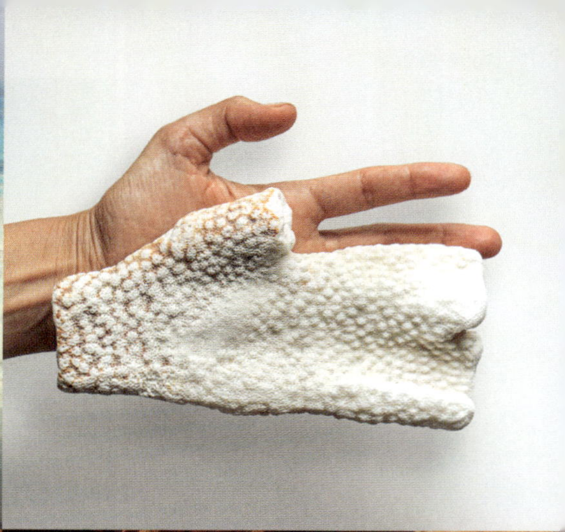

I am fortunate to have grown up among the vast green forests of Finland. Childhood summers were spent tucked away in a hidden cabin, with no running water. Days started with shared family chores: chopping wood for the sauna, pumping water and picking wild blueberries for breakfast. Then I would venture into the archipelago woods – discovering its creatures, listening to its sounds. The evenings brought 'white nights' that never saw the sun leave the sky.

In winter, we experienced the opposite – long, dark days marked only by the sun's quick visit to the horizon. Dark, light; snow, sun; hibernating, awake. Stark seasons like Finland's are a reminder of how nature finds balance, even in contrasts. It was this balance that I had lost.

My solo journey took me back to the Finnish archipelago forests, where I spent weeks at a time exploring my home, seeking the unfamiliar in the familiar. I noticed how mushrooms had sprung from fallen pine trunks, breaking them down to nourish the forest floor, where wood mice foraged for food in the blankets of moss (and one poor soul, panicking at my approach, scampered over my toe!). A woodpecker pecked at a pine cone, gathering seeds and scattering the forest's future. I saw that nothing lives in isolation, rather, every creature depends on many others for food, shelter, procreation. Each being takes, and gives.

I realised that creativity, too, exists as part of a bigger web. It is a force that can feed us, but must also be fed.

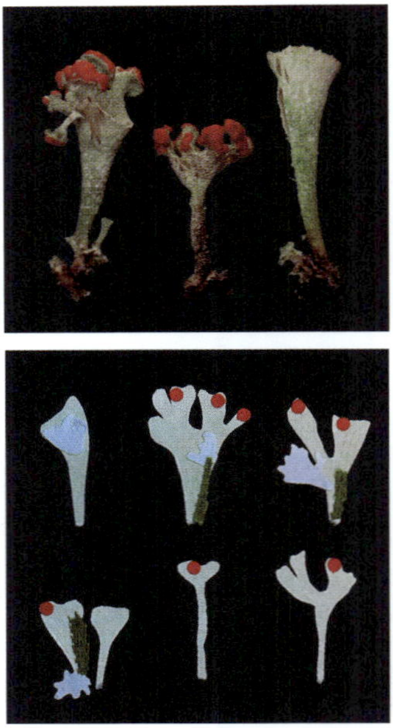

FIELD NOTES
Turku Archipelago lichen, Finland. My source of inspiration for the Creative Ecosystem model.

Right: photo by Jamie Thomas

INSPIRATION
PURPOSE
INTUITION
RESILIENCE
ENERGY

The Creative Ecosystem model

I began to form a new concept: the personal Creative Ecosystem. What inputs does a creative person need to keep their ecosystem in balance? What support, resources and opportunities will feed them?

It is these questions that this book explores, and helps you answer for yourself. For creatives, the demand for output can be constant. It's not often that we take the time to pause and give ourselves the inputs we need.

> The Creative Ecosystem model is a way to think about what balance looks like for you. It covers five areas that act as fuel for creativity: Connection, Wonder, Pause, Movement, Joy.

The experience of each of these – their source, their importance, their availability – is as unique as your creativity. Which is why, in this book, you'll have the opportunity to explore each idea in a way that is personal to you. I'll walk you through prompts and exercises that will help you map out your Creative Ecosystem, and guide you to activate it in your own life.

CREATIVE ECOSYSTEM

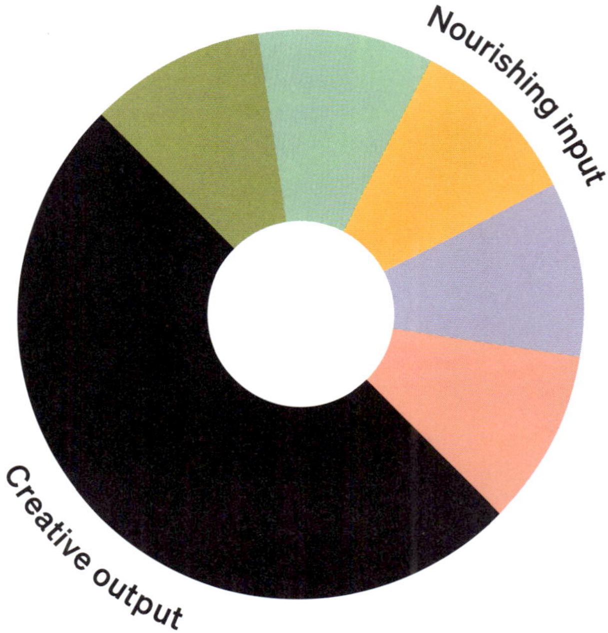

Five core inputs:

Connection **Wonder** **Pause** **Movement** **Joy**

...balance and sustain your creative output by helping you:

Connect who you are with what you do to nurture your **purpose**.

Explore the ordinary with curiosity to nurture your **inspiration**.

Book in time for solitude and reflection to nurture your **intuition**.

Stay fluid and evolve with the process to nurture your **resilience**.

Enjoy immersing yourself fully in an activity to nurture your **energy**.

You are not alone

If you're reading this book, you may already be experiencing some of the signs of burnout. And no wonder: a work culture of late nights and lunchtime meetings, unclear briefs and endless revisions, soon chips away at our wellbeing. Research from consultancy Gallup found that three-quarters of US employees feel burned out at work at least sometimes,[2] and 41% globally report a lot of daily stress.[3]

For those of us who identify as a 'creative', our work often feels core to who we are. If we don't succeed, who are we? The stakes are high, and our wellbeing is the price we pay. Part of this success is income – which is too often low or unreliable, especially for freelancers.

For these reasons I was saddened but not surprised to learn about an Ulster University survey that found that those working in the creative industry are three times more likely to suffer from mental ill health compared to the general population.[4] Anxiety and depression are the most common reported symptoms.

Over the years I have heard stories of people sleeping in their agency's offices, and receiving texts from their boss at midnight. I've been asked to deliver work for free in exchange for 'recognition' because the client is a Fortune 500 company. This focus on output – to produce more ideas, more assets, more quickly – is draining us of what makes us, us.

Signs you might be overworked

You regularly feel overwhelmed or out of energy.

Receiving work emails, even good ones about things you used to be excited about, gives you a sinking feeling.

You often skip exercise and time with friends and family to prioritise work.

You feel guilty when you're not working, even if it's the weekend or you're on holiday.

You check your work email first thing in the morning and last thing before you go to sleep.

You don't remember when you last had a good night's rest.

You skip lunch, start early and finish late.

No amount of planning seems to give you the time you need to be productive enough.

You are finding it difficult to define who you are beyond work.

Are there things you would add to this list?

AT WORK

If you're employed somewhere where you have a manager, talk to them about feeling overwhelmed. Before speaking to them, be clear in your mind on an outcome that would be most helpful for you – whether it's reprioritising tasks, accessing support services, or simply sharing your feelings and being heard. Communicate this with them, and be specific – it helps them give the support you need.

In 2023, I conducted the Creative Wellbeing Insights survey with 58 creatives based across 17 countries.[5] I asked about the biggest challenges they face in their work, and their answers revealed four themes: motivation, management, time and pay.

The pressure to create on demand, coupled with unclear briefs, poor communication, irregular work hours and project management issues, makes managing creative projects complex. And, with limited time for testing out new ideas, it's difficult to push boundaries or find new avenues.

Added to this, there's often a lack of appreciation for creative work, and sometimes insufficient financial compensation. This can make it hard to believe in the worth of our work and, ultimately, our own self-worth.

What do you find most challenging about being a creative?

Staying motivated

"What I find most challenging is the competition present in the industry and the complexity of defining myself as a creative professional in a field in constant flux."

"Managing my own focus and energy."

"Constantly having to come up with interesting ideas! That part seems impossible. Dealing with budgets, having to do more in less time."

"Keeping my motivation up for long periods of time. I am very motivated when I join a new position but I'm usually burnt out in 12–18 months."

Mastering the chaos

"I find managing all of the other stuff that surrounds creativity the most challenging."

"Poor communication from my employer along with their own apathy and ignorance about good design."

"Balancing creativity with logic and research."

"The need to please others and maintain the harmony makes it hard to have a non-hierarchical discussion."

"Managing clients' expectations."

WHAT ARE YOUR
MAIN CHALLENGES
AS A CREATIVE?

Finding time to create

"Having to 'turn creativity on', as if it's a commodity."

"Finding the time to be creative in a world that goes 13,892 km per hour."

"Uncertainty, and living inside a system that doesn't support creatives."

"Setting enough time so that I can be relaxed enough to start something without the end goal looming over the process."

"Finding (paid) work, but still maintaining time for personal projects because those are the best creatively and inspirationally."

Selling the output

"Selling what I do, and putting a price to it."

"Finding clients and promoting myself."

"Communicating what I do."

"Making a living."

"Now the focus is only on revenue, in whatever form possible, strategy doesn't matter anymore, nor do creative opportunities."

How this book will help you

The Creative Ecosystem model is not a tool intended to fix you or bring about quick changes. Rather, it's a tool to help you see and use the resources that are already available to you. It will help you reconnect to the foundation of who you are, and build a fluid system around you to support you through the inevitable bumps in your journey. The tips and exercises we'll walk through together are relevant to you whether you work at a high-profile global design agency or from your kitchen table, and apply to experienced leaders and younger students alike.

Each chapter explores a specific 'input' that can fuel your creativity. And each of these five inputs maps onto one of the five stages of the creative process – Briefing, Research, Ideation, Development and Creation. Using this familiar model, we'll look at new ways to approach challenges in all areas of life.

You may want to keep a notebook on hand so you can jot down your answers to the exercises and refer back to previous ones. Some exercises might feel more challenging than others – that's very normal, and can even hint at which areas of yourself and your life are in need of more focus.

Please note: what I share in this book isn't a substitute for professional help. If you're struggling with your wellbeing, I encourage you to reach out to someone who can support you.

Give each exercise a go, but if some of them don't resonate with you, move on. There's always a different approach waiting for you on the next page. Take what's helpful, leave what's not.

My hope is that you will use what you find in these pages to take the steps you need to fill yourself up – so that you can reconnect with the joy of creativity, now and long into the future.

<u>Insights from creatives</u>
While writing this book, I've delivered talks and workshops on the Creative Ecosystem model in cities all over the world, from Toronto to *Tokyo, Brisbane to Brighton.* I've gathered insights from creatives along the way, shared here as quotes throughout the book.

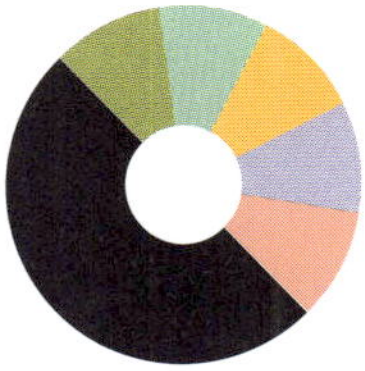

CREATIVE ECOSYSTEM

Five core inputs:

Connection

Think of it like the *Briefing stage*, and it will help you to focus on what matters most to you.

Wonder

See it like the *Research stage*, and it will help you find the unusual in the usual.

Pause

Consider it like the *Ideation stage*, and it will guide your creative spirit.

Movement

Frame it like the *Development stage*, and it will help your mind and body stay flexible.

Joy

Treat it like the *Creation stage*, and it will help you find your spark.

...supported by creative process thinking:

Briefing | Research | Ideation | Development | Creation

...sustain your creative output by nourishing your:

Purpose | Inspiration | Intuition | Resilience | Energy

01
CONNECTION

Connecting to yourself and others helps you sustain your output by strengthening your sense of purpose.

Think of it like the *Briefing stage* of the creative process, and it will help you to focus on what matters most to you.

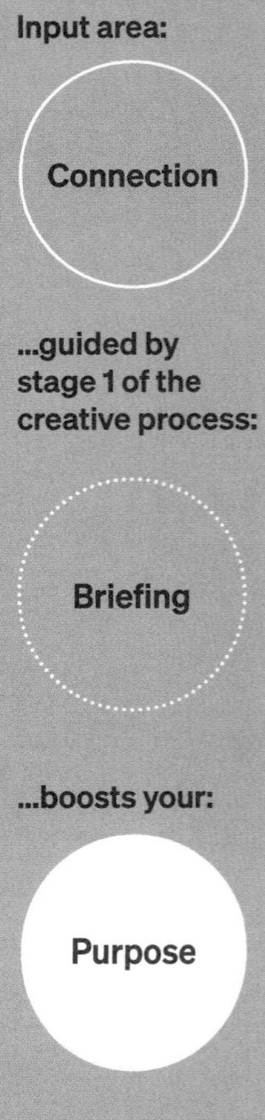

MEANING
SUCCESS
SUPPORT
NETWORK
KINDNESS

How connection creates purpose

Just before I turned 10, I hit upon an inspiring idea. A book in my school library talked about writing a letter to your future self. A simple exercise, but one that did something profound: I could collapse time for a moment, by connecting to different versions of myself. I set to writing myself a letter each birthday, to be opened the following year. When I turned 10, I also wrote a letter to the 20-year-old me.

I love reading back my sticker-laden handwritten notes. The letters are brief, but I ask my future self many questions: Are you still dancing? Do you keep a forest altar? Who do you fancy? Do you like wearing a dress? The letters show me exactly what mattered to the 10-, 11-, 12-year-old Emmi. Even at the time, as I opened each year's letter from the past, they revealed me to myself. Their content anchored me, and showed me the direction I wanted my life to take. Though I sensed my definition of it would evolve over time, I knew I wanted to pursue a simple kind of happiness. I didn't care for shiny riches or grand markers of success; instead, I wanted a cosy place to live, with no big money worries, and enough time to hang out with my friends. Over the years, and with added wisdom, that pursuit has shifted from seeking more immediate contentment to building lasting balance – something that can take years to achieve.

This is what connection can look like, and why it matters. Connection is all about **being you**. It's knowing your story, where you come from, and how this shapes your values.

Just as importantly, it's about building relationships with others who fuel you in ways that matter to you. I have always believed that approaching life with kindness – towards yourself, others and the natural environment – is the best recipe for building a network of joyful, mutually enriching connections. Life proves this to me over and over again.

In this chapter, you'll find prompts that will help you explore and deepen your connections with yourself, and with others. These connections naturally lead you to the heart of what makes you, you. Here you'll find something that so many of us are searching for, and one of the most powerful inputs to our creativity: meaning. You'll start to understand what really (really) matters to you – what your purpose is, and how you might pursue it.

When you lack connection...

...negative thoughts and feelings have an unobstructed path to the forefront of your mind. You might feel detached from your surroundings, or somehow irrelevant to the world. It can feel lonely, or disconcerting. And it can impact every part of life.

Signs you're lacking connection:

You find it difficult to see your own strengths and feel unclear on what you have to offer.

You're hesitant to stand up for what you believe or need, and find it hard to make yourself heard.

You feel there is no meaning or purpose in the projects you spend your time on.

You try to do everything by yourself without asking for help or support.

Guided by the creative process: **Briefing**

To begin your journey of connecting to yourself, we're going to start with something you're likely already familiar with: the Briefing stage.

The creative brief is how most creative projects begin. A good creative brief explains the what, why and how of the project. Which client is it for, and what challenges do they face? Why is the project happening now? What message is it trying to get across, and to whom? What does the team look like, and what's the timeline?

Done well, a creative brief asks questions that get under the surface of the idea and reveal ways it can be improved. It guides you through the creative process, and gives a useful framework for evaluating the work's success later.

> What if you approached your creative self like you would a creative project?

Creating a brief for your creative self is a simple way to ask important questions that will guide you in a meaningful direction. It can help you put your energy in the right places, acknowledge your parameters, and seek the most helpful support.

The alternative, for many of us, is carrying on as we are, grinding our way through each day, each month – letting our focus fall on the things that most loudly demand it, and pursuing goals we're not even sure we set.

So, give it a go. What brief would you give your creative self?

CREATE A BRIEF FOR YOUR CREATIVE SELF

Below are some pointers to get you started. Don't worry if some of these questions feel too big, we'll explore them together in the next pages.

You can come back to these questions anytime you feel a lack of focus or meaning and need a sense of direction.

- What challenges are you facing?
- What would you like to do more and less of?
- What three things matter the most to you in life?
- What are your goals and aspirations?
- What does success look like to you?
- What would you like to avoid?
- Who do you want to positively impact with your actions?
- Who supports you?
- How is your financial wellbeing?
- What three things have shaped your journey?
- Where do you want to be in one year, five years, 10 years' time?

Connect to self

There's a reason I encourage you to look back, to reflect on your journey as a place to start. Perhaps because it's behind us, we often forget our journey has already provided us with many of the relationships, tools, wisdom and other resources that can support us right now.

Many claim they can see Nordic influence in my designs after hearing I'm from Finland. I can't see it myself, but I'm definitely influenced by how methodical the Finns can be. Punctuality, practicality and frankness all seem to come naturally to me. These are hardly creative traits, but they have really helped me run my own creative practice. Not many people can say they enjoy timekeeping – and even bookkeeping!

Looking back on what has shaped us can help guide us into the future. Think of your own cultural roots. These could be traditional practices you grew up surrounded by, family stories you've heard over and over again, or broader cultural norms that you take for granted. How do they influence your work, or even enhance your creativity?

Tracing these threads reveals patterns, and connects us back to what matters to us. During my year-long 'Inspiration Expedition' (I prefer this to 'burnout recovery'), I expected to come back with a single, clear direction guiding me towards the one thing I should do. Instead, I developed an entire system: a Creative Ecosystem. Reflecting on it, this couldn't be more me. I love a good system! It gives me a sense of security, safety, confidence. And sharing that system with others who can benefit from it feels wholeheartedly meaningful to me. I felt everything fit, and knew that taking the Creative Ecosystem out into the world was the right next step for me.

Look back at the past, and we can better map the path ahead.

Catalina Estrada Uribe
Illustrator & Pattern Designer
Colombia

It wasn't until I moved to Barcelona that my roots truly began to influence my work. I started to deeply miss what I had left behind in Colombia – the vibrant colours, the warm light, the music, the jungle. Nature became my muse, my refuge, my sacred place, and I started filling my work with all these things that I missed so much.

Working on social projects for Colombia has allowed me to stay connected to my country. It has introduced me to incredible people who are doing wonderful things. For me, connection is one of my greatest sources of inspiration, and being involved in these projects and connecting with these people has been one of the greatest gifts my profession has given me.

YOUR TIMELINE

Build a picture of your life's journey. Write down positive experiences on the left and negative ones on the right, noting down your age at the time.

Reflect on your experiences. How have they influenced you, shaped your current feelings and guided your behaviour?

SAVOUR THE GOOD. What small moments or bigger experiences are your happiest memories? Who was there, and what felt good about them?

REFLECT ON THE BAD. Which moments or periods of time in your life have been difficult? What was challenging about them – and is there a particular mindset, person or other resource that could support you with something similar in future?

Find meaning

As a young designer, I was hyper-focused on self-expression through visuals. I saw value in bold, politically charged graphics, and not much else. But as the years went by, I started to view myself more as a service provider. My designs help convey a message. The better I do, the wider their message reaches. And the more I believe in the message, the more invested I am in the designs. Bingo! I'd figured out where I found meaning, and I could shift my focus onto work that positively contributed to issues that mattered to me.

We're all looking for meaning in our lives, but where we find it is unique to each of us. It might be purposeful work, community commitments, a spiritual belief system, or a combination of these things. It doesn't matter where you find meaning within your Creative Ecosystem, but it's helpful to figure out exactly where it comes from. You might, for example, find yourself working on a branding project that really motivates you. You arrive at your desk unusually compelled to get started, and find yourself talking about it with friends. The question to ask is: Why? Is there a specific part of the process that's igniting your spark, like interviewing a community group or connecting to new people? Or is there something meaningful to you about the project's role in the wider world, something that fills you with gratitude, or gives you the chance to offer an act of service?

The answer to this question is a clue to where you find meaning. Once you know this, you can pursue more of what matters to you.

When I receive a creative brief, I distil it into keywords that guide me to its essence. Do the same on the following page once you've jotted down the actions, people and feelings that feel good to you. Reflecting on what truly matters helps you follow your inner compass, revealing what's working, and where the gaps are.

Tom Tapper
CEO & Co-Founder
Nice and Serious
UK

Nice and Serious created a democratic decision-making tool called the Moral Compass to make sure we only work with clients and briefs that align with our mission: to make creative work the world needs. Each brief we receive is entered into the Moral Compass and everyone in the team is given an equal and anonymous vote. The system then generates a percentage alignment score. If it's above 50% we can respond to the brief, if it drops below 50% we decline it. On average this means we decline around four briefs a year.

There's a short-term cost to the business from declining projects, but overall I believe this cost is outweighed by the benefits it creates in staff empowerment and brand reputation. It also creates a virtuous circle: we only work on projects that align with our mission, leading to better work, which attracts more of the projects we want.

FEELING GOOD

Write down the activities, people and emotions that make you feel good.

H O W : Good actions

W H O : Good connections

W H A T : Good feelings

CHINAR FAROOQUI

Creative Director

CULTURAL STORYTELLING

For me, Chinar Farooqui's work displays the power and beauty of the threads that connect us to our roots. She's the founder of Jaipur-based clothing brand Injiri, where she creates garments that weave together history, place and craft to carry stories of the past into the present.

How has growing up in rural Rajasthan shaped your perspective on craftsmanship?

I remember accompanying my mother to the old city, where she would visit printing units to buy fabric yardages. Those spaces were alive with the smell of dyes, the sound of blocks hitting cloth, and the hands of craftsmen at work. At home, my grandmother had the most beautiful Jamdani sarees, each one so fine and intricate that it felt like holding a piece of history. It was simply a way of life. Outside our home, craftsmen wove textiles on handlooms, using techniques passed down for generations. These early experiences taught me to see craft not just as a skill but as a form of cultural storytelling. It gave me an appreciation for the rhythm and patience that go into handmade work.

How do the cultural stories embedded in the textiles you work with inspire your collections?

Textiles in India are deeply tied to specific regions, each having its own unique traditions and styles. When we work with a particular weave, like Jamdani, we begin by studying the local vocabulary and the way the craft is used in that region. For us, it's not just about creating something visually appealing; it's about understanding the cultural context and significance of the craft. We prefer to work within the boundaries of that local tradition, because the story behind the weave – the history, the meaning, and its place in the community – is what matters most to us.

Have traditional weaving techniques shaped your design philosophy?

Since the beginning of our work with craft, we've continued to collaborate with the same families, and that relationship has taught us so much about life and working together. Spending time with the craftspeople and observing their weaving process – starching, joining the warp, dyeing – shows us a slower way of life and the sustainable practices still alive in the craft world. We feel lucky that these traditions continue. Watching them teaches us to value slowness and how beautiful things can be made at their own pace. Everyone in the process matters. We learn about simplicity and sustainability from our connection with craft.

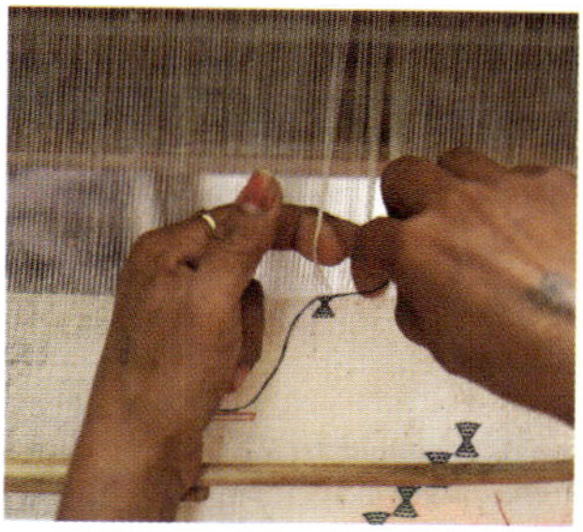

1

2

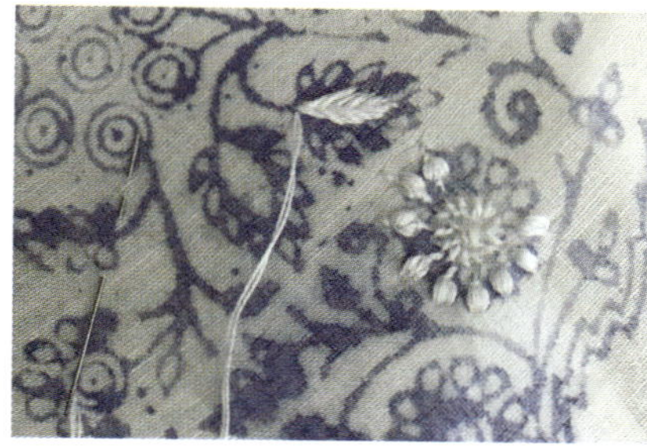

3

4

5

6

TECHNIQUES:

1-2 Bhujodi weave By the turban weavers of Bhujodi

3 Chikankaari Hand embroidery from Lucknow

INJIRI COLLECTIONS:
Photos by Gourab Ganguli

4 Rasa Narrating the comforts and discomforts of our daily routines

5 Nilgiri Inspired by the sensory experience of the spice plantation around the Nilgiri Hills, India

6 TaanBaan Combining ancient Indian techniques of extra weft with intensive clamp dying

Define success

When I set up Studio Emmi two decades ago, it wasn't out of a grand dream to run my own studio – it was because I couldn't find a job. Trust me, I tried. My portfolio was a hand-bound book that took me three days to make, and I'd leave one behind at every studio I visited. Working for myself came out of necessity, not from any great certainty that I had what it takes.

Today, I'm established as a designer, but am I successful? I still compare myself to others, watching friends in agencies grow through teamwork and training. Social media can easily leave me feeling that I'm falling behind. I have to remind myself to define success by my own standards. For me, that means earning from creative work while keeping time for personal projects – a constant balancing act.

For many of us, success is likely to have many dimensions. These might include our relationships with others, personal growth, health, creativity, or being part of something bigger than us. When we think about success in terms of our values, it stops looking like a set of money- or status-driven milestones like owning a new pair of trainers or getting thousands of social media followers. It becomes easier to see it for what it is: an ongoing journey towards the things that enrich our lives. Over time, your definition of success might shift. When it does, rewrite your brief and readjust your goals accordingly.

The trick – and it really is tricky – is to hold on to these bigger ideas about success even in the midst of everyday pressures. When I'm rushing at a project deadline, my sense of success can get myopic: Finish the job! Deliver good work, at all costs! I run the risk of skipping my regular swim, failing to call a friend, or snacking on junk food instead of eating a home-cooked meal. That's a slippery slope. Regular exercise, good food and strong relationships are all part of what real success looks like for me.

Corine Roesner
Transformation Coach
Roes Coach
Australia

A common thing I see is people defining and striving for a success that isn't theirs. It's what they think success should mean, maybe picked up from their parents, peers or society.

Much of the time when we actually break it down, success is hardly ever linked to financial gains or our status in society. These can be important elements, but when we dig deeper, it's what they give us that's actually important. Things such as freedom, family time or giving back. By simply taking the time to tune in and work out what success truly means to you, you'll be aligning with the purpose behind your goals, which can be a power accelerator towards your vision.

List six achievements you are proud of, no matter how big or small.

Remember to celebrate your successes, even the smaller ones. Whether it's going out to dinner to celebrate a milestone or treating yourself to some pampering for keeping up a daily walk for a week, these moments of recognition are important. They remind us that this is what success is. How could you celebrate your achievements above (even if they're in the past!)?

What does being successful mean to you?

When I asked the respondents of my 2023 Creative Wellbeing Insights survey what being successful means to them, their answers were overwhelmingly similar.[6] The details are different but the themes are the same: **as long as our work supports us, and we feel happy and inspired in what we do, we feel we are succeeding.**

Meaningful happiness

"Happiness and being fulfilled in my daily practice."

"Being happy, enjoying what you do. Not focusing on money."

"To be able to make choices that complete me in my professional and personal life instead of choosing one or the other."

"Having meaning."

Making a living

"Being able to do a job that I like and where I'm getting recognition from it, both monetary but also from peers."

"Having enough money to sustain myself, and loving what I do / being happy with what I do."

"Having a business that supports myself and all those I work with creatively and financially."

WHAT'S YOUR DEFINITION OF SUCCESS?

Being part of something

"Making an impact on the life of others, while expressing your true identity and achieving something memorable to yourself and others."

"Influencing change, inspiring others, creating beauty in the world."

"Creating things to share that improve our life on this planet and create communities."

"Serving."

Accomplishing goals

"Ideally, having a seamless thread from doing what I love, to earning a living, and to meaningfully contributing to society."

"Being able to carry out the entire design process with confidence."

"Mental and physical health."

"Looking back at my career and feeling really proud."

"Being able to accomplish your goals and getting the results you wanted."

"Seeing a project fulfil its purpose."

Plan your path

When I arrived in French Polynesia during my Inspiration Expedition, it wasn't because I'd always had my heart set on visiting Tahiti. I had a particular purpose in mind: to explore a landscape that was completely unfamiliar to me and speak with local craftspeople about the challenges they face and what keeps them motivated.

Once I knew that, the decision to take myself to Marquesas and Fakarava took care of itself. I'd made it to my destination by thinking bigger than "where?". Instead, I asked "why?".

Most people don't know exactly where they're going in life. In fact, that would be impossible. Navigating your path in a way that feels good for you isn't about knowing what will happen next. No one can tell you that. It's only ever about taking your next step in the right direction. Your intention – the product of your 'why' – is the compass you need to point yourself in that direction.

What about goals – the tangible outcomes that you know you want to achieve? They, too, can shift as life unfolds. In fact, it's a good sign if they do. If you're checking in with yourself on how well your current goals are aligned with your intentions, there's every chance you'll find yourself revising your goals over time. It's natural to abandon goals that once felt important, because you realise a different goal will lead you in a direction that is truer to your values.

There's no rush to get everything right the first time around. You can reset as many times as you need. If things don't go exactly as planned, don't sweat it. Just take a deep breath, recalibrate and keep moving.

Stefan G. Bucher
Writer, Graphic Designer & Illustrator
USA

As you determine if your Creative Ecosystem is balanced to your liking, when do you take your measurements? If you want to be happy at the end of every day you'll make different decisions than if you want to be happy more often than not over a ten-year span – or if you want to die happy. That one's the riskiest timeframe. It gives you the most time, but if you get it wrong, you're really screwed.

So perhaps the way to a workable balance is to look at your life and your practice through different lenses – today, a year, a decade, a lifetime – at the same time. Experiment with seeing yourself at different points within each timeframe.

Is there still time to change? Is there still time to wait for luck? What timeframes make you happiest?

Goal setting

Hint: look back at page 33, where you listed the people and activities that bring meaning and good feelings to your life. What goals could you set that will give you more of these things?

1. Write down your goal. Be specific: what does achieving this goal look like? And by when do you want to achieve it?

2. Identify a milestone you want to reach along the way. It will help you know that you're making progress.

3. Commit to four specific actions you will take over the next month to make progress towards your goal.

1. GOAL

2. MILESTONE

3. ACTIONS

Manage money

Once upon a time, I was a nineteen-year-old immigrant living alone in a country where I didn't know anyone. I sofa surfed for more than six months, became all too familiar with Britain's humble baked bean, and longed to put my clothes somewhere other than crumpled in a suitcase. It became deeply important to me to know that I would always have a guaranteed place to sleep. Nearly three decades later – with a lot of luck and hard graft – I now enjoy the security of owning my own home.

Those of us working in the creative industries have to deal with a heady mix of financial pressures. Often we're working short contracts at unpredictable intervals, with inconsistent hours and sometimes insultingly low pay. More than half (57%) of US employees say finances are the top cause of stress in their lives;[7] and financial worries can trigger or worsen poor mental health, which can, in turn, impact financial decision-making.[8] The particular challenges of working in the creative industry, and the ways they interact with my own character, mean that I've often prioritised financial security over creativity. At various times, I've chosen lucrative but unexciting opportunities that provided some security, or big projects that paid well but left me no time for my own creative pursuits.

Everyone's relationship with money is hugely personal. Financial decisions, and the role money plays in our lives, run deep. Financial wellbeing is equally complex, and incorporates not only income, but also your management and perception of your finances. Achieving financial wellness means not perpetually worrying about money, and it's an important part of our Creative Ecosystems.

I encourage you to sense check your finances at least monthly, create consistent saving habits, and continue learning about financial management. Use the following exercise to review your budget and get some insight into your feelings about money. Are you avoiding it, do you crave the sense of status it brings, or do you live frugally? How could you build a healthier relationship with money?

Kate Woosey
Financial Planner
UK

The balance between security and the ability to create is complex within the creative process; society has always linked the struggling artist with their creative worth. We often think you can either be creative or mathematical, good with visuals but bad with numbers. This leads many creative people to the notion that they aren't good with money, or they shouldn't be, which can have a negative impact on how we treat our relationship with it.

Like software or materials, money is a tool that creates the foundation that holds up originality, giving the gift of freedom to pursue your passion and create without fear.

CREATE A REALISTIC MONTHLY BUDGET

Monitor your spending habits and create a budget that enables you to live within your means.

Begin by reviewing your income and expenses. Identify your most critical priorities, then allocate funds in descending order of importance.

1. YOUR INCOME

How much money do you receive each month after tax?

Total

2. LIST YOUR EXPENSES

Everything you spend money on each month.

YOUR NEEDS

Fixed expenses like rent, mortgage, groceries, bills, transport etc.

Total

YOUR WANTS

Holidays, shopping, entertainment etc.

Total

Monthly savings (build your buffer).

Payments toward your debts.

3. SUMMARY

INCOME
- EXPENSES
- SAVINGS
- DEBT
=
This is the amount that you have left each month. If it's negative, cut back.

Expenses you could stop or reduce, like cancelling subscriptions.

- [ ]
- [ ]
- [ ]
- [ ]
- [ ]

Connect to others

I've had various studio set-ups over the years – a shared space with a creative collective, a fast-paced agency office, the solitude of my front room. Each arrangement has suited a different stage in my life, yet one constant remains: I need to connect with others, so I don't get stuck in my own head.

Creativity thrives on connections with other minds, whether it's brainstorming with colleagues or a fleeting conversation with someone on the bus. Conversations and experiences with other people give us access to different perspectives, create opportunities to co-operate, and give us much needed emotional support. All these things fuel us to generate ideas and new solutions.

Researchers have found that those who form close connections with someone from a different culture show higher levels of creativity, innovation and entrepreneurship.[9] When we embrace our differences from other cultures, we understand our own culture and others' better. We get a clearer idea of the cultural values and assumptions we're bringing to the conversation, and how we could blend these in new ways with a different view of the world.

Connections are also how serendipity happens. Sharing our goals with the people we're connected to often leads to opportunities that take us closer to achieving them. Early in my career, I fell in love with layout design – I found it such a satisfying way to tell a story by using and reusing elements that guide the reader through the content. I became obsessed with the idea of being able to design a book one day. A whole book! A rare 3D treat for us graphic designers. My experience in layout design was limited, and I didn't have much to showcase. So I turned my whole portfolio into a book, as if to tell the world: "Let me design your book!". I sent it to some contacts, and soon heard from a design studio in New York. They wanted me to design – you guessed it – a book.

So, whatever you're most excited about working on – who could you tell about it?

Émilie Chen
Designer & Art Director
UK/France

In 2016, I co-founded the London chapter of Ladies Wine & Design. As an introvert, I had found big design events intimidating and had struggled to meet people outside of my network, so Jessica Walsh hosting informal chats for small groups in NYC inspired me.

The intimate setting fosters openness and vulnerability, allowing us to share advice on issues like tricky clients and toxic workplaces. The group offers inspiration, reassurance and connections, especially for freelancers seeking community, and for those considering the leap into freelancing. Many, including me, have met collaborators, mentors and close friends... my life would look very different without Ladies Wine & Design.

SAY THANK YOU

Think of a past mentor, or a colleague who has influenced you. Write them a thank you note to express your gratitude for the ways they have helped you. You don't have to send it - but you could!

Nurture connectivity

When was the last time you had a friendly interaction with someone in your neighbourhood, maybe at a cafe or a corner shop? How did it make you feel?

Research shows that people who regularly engage with others, even through brief interactions like greeting a stranger or chatting with a barista, tend to feel a greater sense of life satisfaction.[10] The simple act of connecting with others enriches our lives, and helps us feel like we belong.

When I took Yale University's Science of Well-Being online course, we were encouraged to do something that, at first, made my stomach do a flip flop. Professor Santos instructed us to make one new social connection every day for the next week. It could be chatting with someone while waiting at the traffic lights, striking up a conversation with someone on the bus, or approaching someone new at work.

Strengthening existing connections matters, too: reaching out to a friend you haven't spoken to in a while, or an ex-colleague you lost touch with. When I reflected on the exercise, I remembered what the class had shared: it was uncomfortable at first, but more than worth it. I could see why. My days had more colour in them, and my world felt more connected.

Even the introverted among us can connect with the other beings around us. Nature is full of beings – use the following exercise to connect with them.

INTRODUCING ELEMENT EXERCISES

On the right hand page is the first of five 'Element Exercises' that you'll find in each chapter of this book. These exercises are rooted in one of the five elements – earth, air, ether, water and fire – and help you connect with the concept and mood of each Creative Ecosystem input area on a deeper level. Each element represents a different energy: earth grounds us, air inspires openness, ether holds space for possibility, water flows and adapts, and fire ignites passion. Through these exercises, you'll engage with ideas in a way that is not just logical but also sensory and intuitive.

HOW TO DO THE EXERCISES

1. Find a comfortable spot where you can sit down undisturbed.

2. Settle into your posture. Take a slow deep breath in and out.

3. As you go through the exercise, pause with each step to visualise with your eyes closed or with a soft gaze.

4. Have a pen and paper ready to note down any thoughts or sensations that have come up at the end of the exercise.

ELEMENTS
Visualisation Exercise

EARTH

Imagine that you are in a forest. You're standing still, with your feet rooted firmly in the ground. Sense into it the best you can.

You are surrounded by other trees, and the air smells fresh. Perhaps you hear a bird sing, or wind rushing through the branches.

You feel relaxed and at ease. Most things around you are familiar, although you might spot something new.

You look down and notice the bright green leaves and buzzing bees: it's Summer. Wiggle your toes, and feel how your roots are growing firmer and further into the ground. You are connected to everything around you.

A question arises: "*What* makes you feel rooted?" Another question: "*Who* makes you feel rooted?" The questions repeat, as you feel the answers settling within yourself.

Take a slow deep breath in, and out. Notice whatever answers come to you, and whatever you might smell, taste, see, hear or feel.

Seek support

Everything in my life became easier once I learned to open up and ask for help. And trust me, as a Finn, this didn't come naturally! We're raised to value personal space, quiet reflection and reserved expression over openly voicing our thoughts.

The truth is that none of us are alone, and asking for help is one of the greatest gifts we can give ourselves. Some years ago, I joined a group of six creatives for weekly meetings over Julia Cameron's brilliant guidebook, *The Artist's Way*. As our conversations deepened, I was struck by how similar our worries and concerns were. My feelings were not unique to me. I wasn't alone, and there was no need for me to act like I was. It was one of the best things that has ever happened to me, both creatively and personally.

There's plenty of scientific evidence that shows giving and receiving support is beneficial for our health and wellbeing. Helping others boosts both happiness and self-esteem;[11] and leaning on others for support can improve our health, strengthening our ability to cope with stress and enhancing overall quality of life.[12]

Think of it like this: in design, we carefully put together briefs to make sure we have the right team for the job. The same goes for life – your support system is like that dream team, crucial to the success of your 'project' (you!).

Who are the people who listen to you, inspire you and help you believe in yourself? Turn to these people to start practising the skill of seeking support. Use the space on the right to write down their names.

David Alexander
Creative Director
& Head of Studio
The Frameworks
UK

Creativity and wellbeing are intrinsically linked and my role as a creative leader is to foster both. Two ways I approach this are active and passive support.

Active is weekly catch-ups, in person or via video conference, where it's important we don't just focus on work, plus a weekly mental health check-in where my team scores how they've been feeling and respond to two wellbeing-related questions.

Passive is an 'open door' policy where my team can come to me any time about anything on their mind, personal or work-related. These help me stay connected with my team and their wellbeing.

UPLIFT

Who brings out the best in you and supports your growth? How do they do it, in big or small ways?

LAURA HUNTER

Creative Strategy Director & Founder

CONNECTING PEOPLE

I've worked with Laura Hunter in many capacities over the years, and I'm always in awe of her ability to cut through the noise. She has an instinct for getting to the core message, knowing what to ask, and untangling even the messiest clutter of messages to arrive at something clear and meaningful. As the founder of global talent platform The Now Work, she's building a future of work that prioritises both individual happiness and collective abundance.

How do you identify each person's strengths to connect them with work that's a match for them?

I tend to replace the word strength with passion. At The Now Work, one of our talent screening questions is, "what's your dream impact brief?". That means we look for passion: what fires someone up? What sustainability issue fascinates them? What do they love to do? This helps us identify how someone might suit a brief. In terms of workflows, everyone has unique preferences. Some prefer working alone with space to think, while others thrive in group discussions, debating ideas. Either approach is valid – it's about preference. I also encourage people to know that, while it's good to play to their preferred way of working, it's also important to have empathy for other working styles. Solving big challenges requires groups of people to work together.

How do you cut through the noise during the briefing stage to set clear objectives?

Ask "why?" a lot! I use a reductive approach to get to the fundamentals of the challenge. Creative briefs are usually multidimensional, which is fine. I find that articulating the problem in the most simple language helps to cut out the noise and focus on the task at hand. If you don't do that, you risk burning a lot of energy and creativity on potentially solving the wrong challenge and that can be quite painful.

For those seeking more meaningful connections in their work and personal life, what approaches help?

I've found that having fewer but more meaningful connections works well for me. I'm more on the introversion side of the spectrum and, as a new mum and business owner, am a little time poor. Focusing on building and maintaining deeper connections in my personal life has worked much better for me in this season. And when it comes to work, I'd say the same rings true. At Climate Week New York 2024, we ran a small, private event for chief sustainability officers, facilitating a more meaningful conversation around the challenges of leading sustainability within business. I find those interactions and conversations much more powerful. If you're looking for more meaningful connections in your work life, I'd recommend taking an active role in creating opportunities for those connections to flourish.

How do you sustain a supportive network?

I became a first-time mum soon after launching The Now Work, so this question is particularly pertinent! I'd heard the phrase 'it takes a village' before but had never truly appreciated how true it was. The most effective strategy for me has been learning to ask for help. My mum lives in Yorkshire and I'm in London, so she came once a month for a week at a time to support us. I feel very lucky to have this support system. I think women generally hold a lot in life, but this experience taught me it's okay to admit when you can't hold everything and to ask for help.

What is your definition of success for yourself?

Success to me is having ownership over my time. Ultimately, that's why I became an entrepreneur. I have clients and deadlines to meet, so it's not a complete free-for-all, but I find it liberating to design my day how I want to, and every day can look completely different. I can be there for my son and do the nursery pick-up one day and execute a deal the next. Sometimes there's a trade-off between these things – I don't believe you can have it all at the same time. But the variety keeps life full and colourful!

I defined what success looks like for me through understanding and knowing myself. It took time to get there, and I've been guilty of defining success based on others' expectations. I now know who I am, where I come from, and I'm comfortable with that.

What factors attract and retain top talent in an organisation?

Having a mission that people are galvanised by is important. If people are exchanging their labour for something bigger than shareholder profit, they will be more successful at attracting and keeping top talent in the organisation. Trust is important, too. Trust can manifest in many ways – flexible working being an important one. When people are trusted to do their tasks to the highest standards, on time and on budget, it avoids a culture of micro management that ultimately will lead to brilliant people walking out of the door.

What is the one thing you think we need for a better future of work?

Designing systems and processes that support psychological safety and unlock people's creativity is crucial to a better future of work.

02
WONDER

Wonder helps you sustain your output by giving you new sources of inspiration.

See it like the *Research stage* of the creative process, and it will help you find the unusual in the usual.

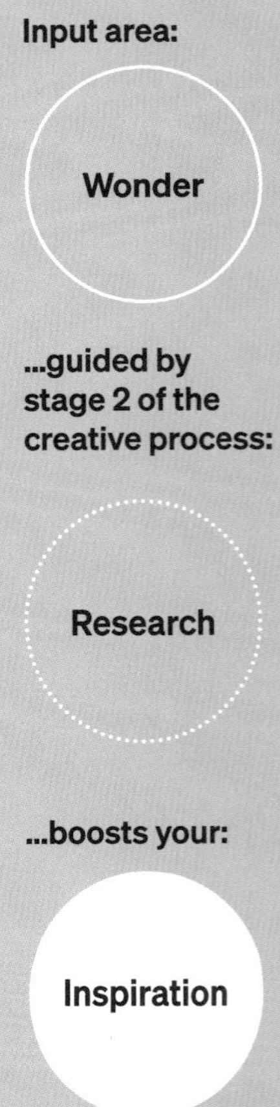

CURIOSITY
SYNCHRONICITY
SHARING
INSIGHT
LEARNING

How wonder leads to inspiration

When I travel, I find myself noticing little things I wouldn't normally. The napkins at the cafe, road signs, floor tiles, trees, hairstyles. Everything looks different, new, interesting – it's fun to feel that sense of surprise. Supermarket aisles become the ultimate source of wonder, and I get shamelessly excited about the typography on flour packaging.

It's much harder to feel this kind of unexpected delight in the familiarity of everyday life. That said, I've discovered that, with a bit of curiosity, it's always possible to find the unusual in the usual. Unpredictable opportunities crop up when I keep my mind open. The more willing we are to let the unfamiliar influence us, the more creative and surprising the outcomes can be.

Today I noticed how the hourglass on my desk shifts between yellow and orange hues with the changing sunlight. It made me consider how my mood changes over the course of the day, and how I can relate it to the same colours. That got me thinking about how I could record it, and perhaps turn it into a diary.

Sometimes small daily observations can grow into life-changing realisations. One day on a walk in the Finnish archipelago forest, I picked up a piece of moss. I've walked on the forest's dense carpet of moss for many years, since I was first able to step into my wellies – but I hadn't ever considered looking at this tiny, fluffy forest dweller up close. It was full of life! Among its small green fronds, an entire micro-ecosystem thrived. Moss, I soon learned, is home to countless microorganisms, tiny creatures like mites and water bears, and even symbiotic fungi. Each plays a role in the delicate balance of life in this soft, hidden world. And mosses, in turn, support the health of the forest by retaining moisture and enriching the soil.

It was the beauty and balance of the moss that gave me the idea on which the Creative Ecosystem model is based: nothing exists in isolation, least so our creativity. Everything is in relationship with everything else. By **staying curious**, we can notice the nature of these connections. When we do, we can't help but be inspired.

When you lack wonder...

...the world around you can seem flat and colourless, as if each day is the same. You might feel like life has become stagnant or devoid of sparkle, and it's hard to engage or be interested. It might feel like emptiness, indifference, or apathy towards any or all parts of life.

Signs you're lacking wonder:

You're stuck in an uninspiring routine, repeating patterns that no longer spark feelings of joy or curiosity.

You settle for less out of fear of failure.

You avoid uncertainty, steering clear of situations where the outcome isn't clear.

You become overly focused on the past or anxious about the future, losing sight of the magic in the present moment.

Guided by the creative process: **Research**

To discover and deepen wonder in yourself, we're going to use a simple method that mirrors step two of the creative process: the Research stage.

Once we have a creative brief in place and know our direction, the next step is research. We gather all the relevant information we can find – reading, speaking to people, visiting places – to guide the creative direction of the project. Who are we creating this for? What do we want to say or achieve? What is happening in this area right now and what ideas or examples can inspire us? How will what we learn guide our work?

We can do research by collecting data, conducting interviews, putting together moodboards or looking at reference books. We analyse the findings to extract meaningful insights. Carried out successfully, research gives us a well-informed foundation that helps make sure the final output is relevant, impactful and aligned with the project goals.

> Research isn't just useful. It also trains us in a mindset that can get us closer to feelings of wonder.

When we research for a new project, we are still open to any direction and outcome. It's a non-judgemental way of looking at the world, in search of brand new knowledge or unexpected quirks. I love this stage – it's an opportunity to rummage through my ever-growing collection of reference images, collected over many years. It's like its own little adventure.

To be struck by inspiration, we have to have an open mind and be ready to see connections in unexpected places. Cooking dinner, walking in the park, wandering round the supermarket – all are an opportunity to exercise curiosity.

On the right is my colour research. When colours in my day-to-day line up nicely, I take a picture and create a colour palette, then save them to my colour reference folder.

What catches your eye in everyday life that you could collect to create your own reference library?

Habits—and Changing Them
Beck

The wonder in you

Although I follow a Monday to Friday working week, being self-employed for me is all about flexibility. I run errands when I need to, perhaps do an exercise class in the middle of the day and sometimes choose to work on a Saturday to get uninterrupted thinking time away from calls and emails.

This flexibility gives me what I need to make the most out of each day. I used to value the weekends more as 'my time', but I've learned to be more present even on a Monday. I take great pleasure in using my geranium hand cream, selecting my morning coffee cup, and enjoying fresh towels in the bathroom. There's magic in routine. If we can appreciate small moments in our daily grind, we can tap a wellspring of inspiration.

If I pay attention, I can see the beauty of a tiny new leaf growing on my plant. Or notice that the colours of the dishes on the drying rack match perfectly! And is that the first spring sunshine warming my cheeks? The more mindful we are, the more curious we grow.

Boredom is becoming an alien concept in our age of smartphones and social media, but it can be fertile ground for creativity.[13] When we're bored, our mind wanders, and we start making connections between ideas. So, take the opportunity to be still – to slow down, to notice details you'd normally overlook.

In noticing details, you might also start noticing synchronicities. Synchronicity is when coincidences happen that can't be explained, but feel meaningful. If you completed the goal-setting exercise in the previous chapter, you might now be noticing cues in your everyday life that relate directly to your goals. Right in front of you, just previously overlooked. What a funny thing!

Rob Duncan
Creative Director
Mucho
USA

Always look for the gift. I was taught this by John Rushworth, a partner of Pentagram London when I was lucky enough to work there in 2000.

When it comes to branding and logos in particular, always try and find the gift – that clever idea, negative space, twist of a letter. It's about really looking, not just seeing. Study what is already there in the shape of the letters or a symbol and give it an unexpected twist.

There's an 'aha' moment when the client and their customers notice the idea. It raises a smile, almost like getting the punchline in a joke.

MIX 'N' MATCH THE MUNDANE

Find inspiration in the mundane by looking at everyday things with fresh eyes.

1.

Write down three lists of everyday things you notice:

OBJECTS	PLACES	ACTIONS
Things you see or use (a chair, a kettle, a book).	Spots you visit (a supermarket aisle, a park bench, a bus stop).	Things you or others do (walking the dog, waiting in line, sipping coffee).

2.

Randomly pick one item from each list and combine them. Then let your imagination play. For example:

Object: A kettle
Place: A bus stop
Action: Waiting in line

Idea: "A pop-up tea stall at a bus stop that turns waiting in line into a social moment."

3.

Explore the idea and use your combination as a springboard for creativity:

Storytelling prompt
Who are the people stopping for tea? What conversations might start here?

Design prompt
How could the tea stall be designed to make waiting in line more enjoyable?

Creative exercise
Sketch or write about the atmosphere at this pop-up tea stall.

Feel, hear, see, taste, smell

Noticing details isn't just about looking. There's so much in our day-to-day lives that we can discover if we use all our senses. Listen deeply. Feel closely. Savour scents. Taste thoughtfully.

My partner and I once rented a house in the Portuguese countryside. All was as expected until we entered the 'adega', a cellar-like space for winemaking. This one, unusually, had a hatch in the floor. Without hesitation, my partner opened it – and found a deep, dark hole that we couldn't see the bottom of.

Instead, we explored using sound. We tested the echo of our voices, then dropped small stones and heard them land with a watery splash. We figured out that the hole was a natural crevice well, covered with a concrete floor and an access opening. We kept making sounds, and listening to them bounce back, copying themselves, receding into the distance.

The invisible sound-world we had created in the well reverberated through my imagination. I found myself taking new turns on existing trains of thought: what is lost when a message is passed along? What are the ripple effects of small actions? Sensing the world in this unusually focused way had given me a new way to experience and explore my reality.

I love this memory, of the strange well in the stone house. It feels special – because it is, but also because I experienced it through hearing and feeling instead of seeing. Using all of our senses to explore the world enriches our perception, deepens our understanding and makes everything more vivid.

Lauren Davies
Senior Strategist &
Sensory Designer
HEKA
UK

I am passionate about exploring food preparation by engaging all my senses – taste, smell, sight, hearing and touch. The aromas ignite my imagination, transporting me to faraway places, while vibrant colours evoke joy and help me refine my visual style.

The sounds ground me in the present, and the tactile process deepens my connection to intuition. By immersing myself in the anticipation of flavour and the sensory richness of food, I nourish both my creativity and sense of wellbeing. This multi-sensory experience is a powerful and fulfilling personal form of expression.

SENSE YOUR SURROUNDINGS

Write down:

5
things
you see

4
things
you touch

3
things
you hear

2
things
you smell

1
thing
you taste

Use your five senses to explore a new idea you're researching. What would your idea sound like? Taste like? Feel like?

BOOK IMMERSION As you hold this book, feel its weight and texture. Focus on its smell, and the sound when pages turn.	TASTE FOCUS Taste different coloured foods (like red berries or green vegetables). How do you think their colour has influenced your experience of their taste?	SOUND MAPPING Close your eyes, and sketch out a map of your surroundings using just the sounds you hear, marking where different noises come from.
THERMAL SENSING Notice the temperature differences between objects you touch.	SCENT RECALL Find three different scented things - like spices, or flowers - and smell them. Can you bring to mind a memory linked to each one?	COLOUR HUNT Look around the space where you're sitting, and choose a colour. Now, find as many shades of that colour as you can.

Navigate boundaries

As much as I encourage you to keep an open mind, I'm also a huge fan of setting boundaries. Learning to navigate these dualities can spark something unexpected. Try being open; now try to set a limit.

It's much like a blank piece of paper. It's so vast, and so... blank. When I'm free to jot down anything, it can feel debilitating. Where do I start? But given a framework to work within, I soon find ideas begin to flow freely. Guided by a creative brief, my framework might look something like: "Only note down ideas that remind me of a friendship." Suddenly inspiration is all around me. A pair of chairs. An open book. A framed photo. Two puzzle pieces. All become symbols of a friendship and end up in my sketchbook.

By removing the distraction of infinite choice, I can focus on experimenting deeply within the constraints I have set.

Use this trick of setting constraints to go further in your journey of uncovering the unexpected in your day-to-day routine. Each day, apply a rule to your everyday activities – take a different route to work, for example, or dress only in one colour. Listen to music from a specific continent, or eat only raw food. Notice the feeling of newness these limitations create.

Boundaries are also helpful in another way: they can be vital for our wellbeing. The kinds of boundaries that reflect our understanding of our own needs – when we need a rest or a lunch break, when we need alone time or an evening off – are important to notice, and to communicate. It's a case of prioritising, and allowing your needs to come first. This could look like saying: "Yes, I'd love to take on the task, but I can't meet the deadline. If it can wait a month, I'm available." The results are the same either way. Both creative and personal boundaries can energise and inspire us.

June Mineyama-Smithson
Artist & Design Lecturer
Japan/UK

I believe inspiration is everywhere, waiting to be uncovered – like a child playing hide and seek. In my 'Apple Workshop', I ask my students to observe a single ordinary apple. The challenge is to uncover as many colours, patterns, connotations and personal memories as possible. You'd be surprised how much inspiration you can draw from an everyday fruit.

After this exercise, I encourage everyone to go out and explore, because you'll start to see the world differently. Neuroscientist Dr. Tara Swart explains this idea 'value-tagging' in her book *The Source* – the brain's process of assigning importance to certain information. Your brain becomes primed to find inspiration, noticing what you hadn't before and connecting the dots in new and unexpected ways.

SET LIMITS

Practise creating and working within different kinds of boundaries.

JOURNAL

For one week, write down moments of discomfort or overextension that you experience. Note down how a boundary might have helped, and how you might express it to someone else.

VISION

Create a visual board with images, quotes or keywords that reflect the boundaries you want to strengthen.

YES?

When pressured to say “yes”, pause and consider your boundaries. Write responses to protect your time, like suggesting another timeline or saying “no”. Use what feels right.

TIME

Sketch something around you, but give yourself only one continuous line and one minute.

WORDS

Sketch an object while repeating only three words aloud (e.g.“bold, round, loud”). Then draw it again with no word limits.

SCALE

Draw the same object twice: once to fill the entire page, and once using only a tiny box in the corner.

Deepen your voice

During one of my regular meet-ups with other creatives, a designer friend of mine called Dana brought up a worry that had been playing on her mind. "I don't have a voice," she said to us. "Everyone is talking about a voice and I don't have one!" I couldn't believe what I was hearing. Having worked with her for years, to me it was plain as day what makes her output uniquely hers. Why couldn't she see it too?

I realised that everyone else in our small creative group has been led by a passion for sustainable design, which has given us an easily definable 'stamp' across all our work. Dana doesn't share this particular passion – and because of that, she had started to believe that there was nothing distinct or recognisable about her work.

If this is something you relate to, ask yourself: "What excites me?" All of us feel passionate about something – whether it's mountain climbing, classical music, race cars or spicy food. Have a think about where your excitement comes from. And then dive in! Marvel in it, celebrate it, talk about it, share it. Let it absorb itself into your conversations, your choices, your work. Feel your confidence build around what it feels like to be authentically yourself.

My friend Dana has a distinct way of creating decorative visual identities. She crafts layered tapestries of type, colour and imagery that tell stories, and can be applied to anything from business cards to billboards. She spends her weekends at art exhibitions, collects colourful textile references and spots patterns everywhere she goes. Somehow she had separated this passion from what shaped her creative voice.

Your voice isn't a monologue. It is an ongoing conversation with the beauty of the world within us and around us, that leaves a unique stamp on what we create. And even without knowing it, my friend is a master at it.

Kevin Finn
Brand Expert & Author
TheSumOf
Australia

For eight years I thought about starting an independent design journal. I envisioned the publication being led by writing, not visuals, because I was more interested in the ideas surrounding our field.

At the time, this wasn't a common idea within the design community. In fact, I frequently talked myself out of pursuing it. Why? I felt unqualified. I wasn't a writer, interviewer, editor or publisher. Who was I to attempt something this significant? But in 2003, I finally changed my mindset and did something so easy, yet remarkably difficult: I gave myself permission.

My design journal was called Open Manifesto, and for the next 15 years, it featured interviews and essays from some of the most significant designers in the world, alongside influential global thinkers. It changed my life and saved my career.

If you're blocking yourself from pursuing something you're passionate about, give yourself permission – and ask one simple question: Why not me?

BE IT, SPEAK IT

Get in touch with your voice, and explore the conversation you're having with the world.

1

Write 10 "I love" statements that capture who you are, such as "I love roots reggae music" or "I love standing in lavender fields".

2

Think about how each statement could influence your creative style, content, or approach.

For example, if you've written "I love lavender": how could you integrate purple into your work? Or the scent of flowers? Or a calmer way of creating?

Trust it, explore it, embrace it.

EMILY FORGOT

Designer & Artist

FINDING INSPIRATION

British artist and designer Emily Forgot's work never fails to spark my curiosity, and Emily herself is a real inspiration. We've collaborated on some wonderfully whimsical dream projects, and I'm always struck by her vast visual research library, her generosity in sharing ideas, and her sharp eye for reinterpreting the past.

How do you find wonder?
There's too much to inspire me! Every project I do unearths new inspiration or discovery. Each project starts with a digging process – in fact, the research is my favourite part. How it feeds into a final piece can vary greatly but I would say it's important to have a wide range of influences. It's the mix of influences you discover in the moment and those you have nurtured over time and alongside your personal and unique creative nature that enables you to create something… not necessarily original but hopefully authentic.

We used to get together in a group over *The Artist's Way* book on a weekly basis. What did those meetings mean to you?
It was a way of engaging with my creative self that I had never given myself the permission to do before. It felt incredibly reflective and really made me think deeply about what I wanted to make and why. The group element to reading the book and taking part in the exercises together was equally important. We often write plans down and have ideas in our heads about projects but by sharing them with others, saying aspirations out loud they can almost begin to have a life of their own.

Have you ever lost your spark?
It helps to get outside of myself when I feel like this. Seeing the amazing work from history seems to get my creative juices flowing again. Travel, too. Being in new places helps your eyes to see in new ways, to make new connections, to get excited about simple things like colours and textures, designed and undesigned. When I can't travel I love giving myself time to go down the internet rabbit hole. I also think a lack of confidence can get in the way of ideas coming to fruition. But perhaps it's important to feel a bit flat sometimes. If you loved what you made and saw no reason to improve, you would remain stagnant, producing the same things over and over again, and never challenging yourself and developing… that's another way to look at it.

How do you balance your Creative Ecosystem?
This is a work in progress. I think it has so much to do with boundaries that I am setting more. We all need to carve out time at least once a week to do something that energises us creatively.

1

2

3

4

1-2 Emily's inspiration research and moodboards

3 Our House, Our Home Table for De Bijenkorf, photo by Yvonne Witt

4-5 Bricolage and Kiosk Installations for Brookfield Properties, photos by Ruth Ward

6 Trappenhuis Rug for De Bijenkorf made in collaboration with Floor Story

5

6

The wonder around you

Opening up our minds and our senses can help us escape linear thinking, and notice different possibilities. I think of it like the wind: moving, gathering pace, then calm again; lifting things up in the air then placing them down somewhere else. I try to keep the fresh air moving in my mind – to open up a mental window to air it out. I also air thoughts and discoveries by sharing them with other people, letting conversation shape and invigorate them.

For me, the feeling of wonder comes most reliably from nature. When the stars are bright in the sky and I have a rare clear view away from the city's light pollution. When I find a standing dead tree in the Archipelago forest, and it turns out to be full of new life, with a bird's nest tucked inside its hollow trunk. And that one, extraordinary time a humpback whale swam alongside me in the middle of the South Pacific Ocean. I'm still not sure if I was more scared of the depth of the sea, or the size of the whale. Both were humbling.

These feelings – of reverence, admiration, wonder – belong to a powerful emotion that humans have always felt, but scientists have only recently defined: awe.[14] Awe can feel profoundly moving, and often includes a feeling of respect, even fear.

Awe can also shape our perception of time. Research shows that experiencing awe can lead us to feel that we have more time and to feel less impatient.[15] Research participants who experience awe are more willing to volunteer their time, prefer experiences over material goods, and feel more satisfied with life. Scientists attribute this to the fact that awe brings us fully into the present moment – which, in turn, can boost feelings of life satisfaction.

Awe often arises when we encounter something vast, surprising or beautiful. By keeping our minds open and receptive to these experiences, we're more likely to get a chance to bask in moments of life-affirming, wellbeing-boosting awe.

Chris Bolton
Designer
Finland/UK/Canada

I find unexpected insights when I step outside, do everyday things, or pause with music. When I give myself a little space to breathe, curiosity takes over. That's when I make fresh connections and I start to see things differently.

ELEMENTS
Visualisation Exercise

AIR

Find a spot where you feel comfortable and light. Perhaps near a window, outside on a balcony, or in front of a gentle fan circulating fresh air. Take a few deep breaths, letting the air in your lungs energise you.

Imagine yourself high on a mountaintop, surrounded by vast open sky. Feel the air moving around you, light and expansive. Let your thoughts float by like clouds. As you breathe deeply, let the air carry away any heavy thoughts, creating space in your mind. With each inhale, take in clarity. With each exhale, let go of any limits or doubts.

Now, reflect on three areas: self, surroundings and possibilities. Ask yourself three things:
Self: “How open am I to new experiences?”
Surroundings: “What do I notice in my surroundings that inspires wonder?”
Possibilities: “What possibilities am I open to discovering?”

When you’re ready, bring yourself back to the present, carrying this sense of openness with you. Open your eyes, take a few breaths, and jot down any thoughts or feelings that surfaced.

Explore near and far

I've taken days, weeks and even months to travel in search of awe. I have found it where I expected to: in the vibrant underwater life of the Great Barrier Reef; in the sacred rocks and ancient trees of Mount Mitake's mystical forest; in the enduring traditions of New Mexico's revered Pueblo communities.

But I've also found it in surprising places. Awe doesn't only exist in faraway lands, and travel doesn't have to mean crossing oceans or borders. Exploring locally – in your overlooked neighbourhood park, the unfamiliar corner of your city, or even the street you usually hurry down – can reveal hidden beauty when approached with curiosity. Finding awe is not about where you go, but how you look.

A bustling city street can be as inspiring as a remote atoll if you pay attention to the rhythm, colour and stories unfolding around you. Notice the details others might pass by. When you look with intention, a common daisy peeking between the pavement stones can be as beautiful as a rare orchid.

Exploration, by its very nature, requires us to step out of our comfort zone. Even just a little bit. Trust yourself, and see how capable you are of facing the unfamiliar. Walk into that book shop you normally walk past; sign up to that life drawing class; book a solo trip to a city you've never been to. Get out there, and find the inspiration that's waiting for you.

Sam Furness
Founder
Channel Twelve
& Creative Quests
UK

I'm committed to a personal creative practice I call 'Questing'. It involves setting a theme for one calendar month and letting that theme shape your experience of day-to-day life. Imagine that the month was colour themed: What creative experiments might you undertake? What books might you read? What events would you go to? It's a learning journey, a lifestyle experiment, a creative process.

Over nine years and 30+ themes (inc rewilding, time, movement, sculpture) I've learned the incredible power of 'intentional curiosity', which I define as "consciously seeking new perspectives – beyond the boundaries of your experience, past interests, or beliefs".

When we choose to be curious about something, we weave intention into everything we do. As a result, we create a sort of magnetic field around that subject. We go to new places. We try new things. We seek out passionate people. We notice often overlooked details in our environment. We begin to feel like we are in conversation with the world around us, where our curiosity and questions are met with inspiration and a profound sense of connection.

FIND ADVENTURE

Experiment with simple ways to make everyday experiences feel like a new adventure.

TRAVEL LOCALLY

Adopt a tourist's mindset: pretend you're visiting your area for the first time. What do you notice?

-- WISH YOU WERE HERE --

Walk instead of drive. Take a new route. Pause to observe and appreciate what's around you.

* SUNNY LOCAL *

Visit local markets, museums or cultural events in your area. Who can you strike up a conversation with?

GREETINGS FROM THE GREEN

Take a walk in a park, along a river or through a woodland. Or simply spot how much green is growing between the pavement stones.

x
EVERYDAY WITH LOVE
x

Pick out a detail you've never noticed before in your daily routine. It could be a bus stop you often walk past, or the font used on your washing machine.

CREATIVE SOUVENIRS

Like a traveller gathering keepsakes, find different ways to note down your explorations.

Sketch shapes, textures, shadows, scenes, patterns.

Collect tickets, leaves, labels, colours, sounds, smells, snippets of overheard conversations.

Record short voice memos as walking reflections.

Map your route and mark where something caught your attention.

What inspires you?

In my Creative Wellbeing Insights survey, I asked creatives: what inspires you?[16] The answers revealed an incredible diversity in the ways creative people wholeheartedly immerse themselves in the world.

More than nine out of 10 (91%) said that they find inspiration in their everyday lives.

Space and time

"A good night's sleep!"

"Family and proper time away from work, out of the country. The sea."

"Time to dwell on ideas."

"I plan artist dates for myself and day trips to explore areas of my city."

"The quiet."

Change and the new

"A change of scene to explore something or somewhere new."

"The next job!"

"People, places and experiences."

"Travelling and experiencing different places and communities."

"Movement, big dreams, collective energy, connections and change."

Creative practice

"Just an innate feeling of wanting to create."

"Making things with my hands."

"I am directly inspired by seeing other people's work that I admire and their attitude and energy used to fight for its purity."

Learning and growing

"Generally being immersed in creative culture, whether that's in design, music, art, architecture."

"Feeling a sense of progress."

"Visiting museums is my happy place that always keeps me looking forward to create new things."

"Discovering new technologies, education, collaborations."

Mama Earth

"Nature and being surrounded by it."

"A new day, a new sunrise, the moon."

"Everything outdoors."

"Being in the sea and mountains at least a couple times a year."

Everyday things

"Everything around me."

"Meaningful conversations."

"Beautiful stories."

"Talking to my family."

"Music, people, walking, doing, being."

WHERE DO YOU FIND INSPIRATION?

Ask why

Why do leaves change colour in autumn? Why does music make us feel emotional? Why do we light candles for special occasions? As children, we were so good at endlessly asking: "Why?" Perhaps you still remember what fascinated you most as a child. Childlike curiosity is just as valuable to us today, as adults – and can help us embark on our next voyage of discovery.

On my travels, I met Karsten Vestergaard, Programme Coordinator for Visual Communication at DMJX in Denmark. He shared with me the Everlearner model, which he developed to shift the focus from tools-based learning – the kinds of practical skills that you can often learn online – to the deeper art of learning *how* to learn.

This shift can help all of us navigate today's fast changing world. The Everlearner model is all about adopting a mindset based in curiosity, adaptability and self-reflection – everything we need for lifelong growth.

Research indicates students often don't ask questions because they fear being judged.[17] None of us wants be wrong. I certainly don't! Too often, I wake up in the night worried that I've made a mistake or overlooked something.

But creativity needs room to explore. It needs the freedom to poke, test, ask – to get it wrong. Creativity thrives in spaces where we can question without fear and embrace the unexpected.

Mistakes are not failures, but rather a signal that you're exploring properly. Give yourself permission to ask questions, open doors and learn more – even if your path is paved with missteps and errors. Having this freedom is the only way we can learn.

Karsten Vestergaard
Programme Coordinator
DMJX
Denmark

I developed the Everlearner to help students embrace lifelong learning. It isn't just about staying current, it's about understanding yourself as a learner. I encourage students to observe their progress by asking, "Where were you on Monday? Where are you today, this Friday?". This helps them focus on their journey, not compare themselves to others.

The Everlearner combines study, practice and exploration, going beyond mastering tools to developing resilience and creativity. As technologies evolve, this approach ensures students adapt and grow, rather than becoming rigid. In a fast-paced world, slowing down to learn deeply is essential. By fostering curiosity and critical thinking, we prepare students to excel as lifelong learners.

WHY?

Because

WHY?

Because

WHY?

Because

WHY?

Because

WHY?

Because

GO DEEPER WITH THE FIVE WHYS

An important aspect of the Everlearner model is the practice of asking what Karsten calls 'critical questions'.

Get started by diving deeper into a central question: "Why?" This exercise helps to uncover hidden motivations, ideas and barriers. Here's how.

IDENTIFY A CHALLENGE OR GOAL
Start with a specific question, like, "Why am I struggling to come up with new ideas?"

ASK "WHY?" TO DIVE DEEPER
Each 'Why' reveals underlying thoughts or emotions.

For example:

1. *Why do I feel uninspired?*
   I'm stuck in a routine.
2. *Why am I stuck in a routine?*
   I don't take time to explore new things.
3. *Why don't I explore new things?*
   I feel like I don't have the time.
4. *Why do I feel like I don't have the time?*
   I prioritise work over creative exploration.
5. *Why do I prioritise work?*
   I worry about falling behind.

Here, the root cause for being uninspired is a fear of falling behind.

Once the root cause is clear, take action. For example: start your day by jotting down three things you're proud of from the last five years – big, small, work-related or not.

Based on the Five Whys technique, developed at Toyota by Sakichi Toyoda.

Float ideas

Through the ages, we have gathered around campfires to share stories, dreams and ideas. Today these conversations can happen anywhere: a cosy cafe, a bustling kitchen table, in the palm of your hand.

When I'm asked to talk at design conferences or creative festivals, I'm always excited to share my ideas with people on stage. What I really look forward to, though, is the chance to meet other people. It's the conversations I have after the talk that fuel my inspiration for months.

Not least because these conversations give me a peek 'behind the scenes' of someone else's creative process – especially when I've seen their work before. "Oh, that's why your writing is so smart and ironic, it's because you're hilarious!" Not to mention how comforting it is to hear the challenges others have faced and overcome. It eases my insecurities to know they, too, feel overwhelmed by yet another email on a bad day.

You don't need to wait for a conference to find your creative family. Earlier in this chapter, I asked Emily Forgot to reflect on our book club, which I also discuss on page 48. There were six of us, and each week we gathered at someone's house to share food while working through a book and talking about the emotions and realisations it sparked. Could you gather a small group to do the same, online or in person?

Research suggests that some moments of creativity arise in a group setting in ways they can't when we're alone – and that it could be as relevant to think about how others can help boost our creativity, as it is to think about our solo creative explorations.[18]

Matthew Haynes
Founder
The Design Conference
Australia

I believe that being creative is the same as participating in a sport that has no rules. So in creating the rules, we also create new and exciting ways of thinking.

And should you be brave enough to share these thoughts with your peers and colleagues, you may find your contribution is the catalyst for concepts and ideas that are much more significant than you ever imagined. I encourage it.

WAYS TO SHARE AND LEARN FROM OTHERS

Start a storytelling circle

Sign up to workshops

Throw an idea party

Host a curiosity walk

Create a mini zine

Create a collaborative mural

Start a 'question of the week' group chat

WHAT DO YOU WANT TO LEARN ABOUT?	WHAT COULD YOU TEACH OTHERS?

ANNA STARMER

Colour Specialist & Forecaster

SHARING WONDER

I'm totally in love with colour, and I look to Anna Starmer with deep admiration for how she sees the world. Her eye for hues feels instinctive, like she's uncovering something hidden in plain sight. As Founder and Creative Director of Luminary, a global colour forecasting guide, she is a true colour treasure hunter. Through colour, she explores the world with curiosity and is reimagining design for our collective future.

How do you encourage discovery in your storytelling?

I create visually stunning narratives that provoke curiosity and inspire bold decisions. Storytelling, for me, is about connecting deeply with colour as an emotional, instinctual experience, one that sparks new ideas and drives meaningful conversations. Through my publication Luminary and years of global research, I guide designers to embrace innovation while considering the Earth's resources and our interconnectedness. My aim is not just to inspire but to empower others to make thoughtful, transformative choices.

How do you gather insights?

I gather insights through a deeply personal and intuitive process, always starting with colour. Inspiration is everywhere – local and global, physical and virtual. I find it in books, podcasts, art galleries, travel, conversations with customers, and discussions with peers on global colour panels. Often the objects I find inspire me – flowers, stones, fabrics, or paint shades that captivate me with their texture or hue. My studio is a treasure trove of these discoveries, alongside images I've collected from art, fashion, architecture and food. This eclectic mix shapes the ideas and themes I explore further.

To bring these ideas to life, I work with textile dyers to create exact fabric swatches, often experimenting with natural dyeing techniques – using foraged plants, grape skins or coffee grounds. These colours spark conversations and challenge designers to rethink how they create, encouraging thoughtful innovation in their processes.

Looking to the future, how do you find emerging trends?

My research reflects the current political and emotional zeitgeist while building new and disruptive narratives. It's not just about colour; it's about addressing the transformations we face as a society. Looking ahead, I believe trend forecasting must focus on creating hopeful, thoughtful connections. Each decision should consider its impact, turning actions into meaningful contributions to our planet and its future.

1

2

3

4

5

6

1-2 Anna in her studio with work in progress

3-4 Luminary Issue 30, LOVE

5 Luminary colour swatches

6 Hibiscus pigment

03
PAUSE

Pausing helps you sustain your output by strengthening your intuition.

Consider it like the *Ideation stage* of a creative process, and it will guide your creative spirit.

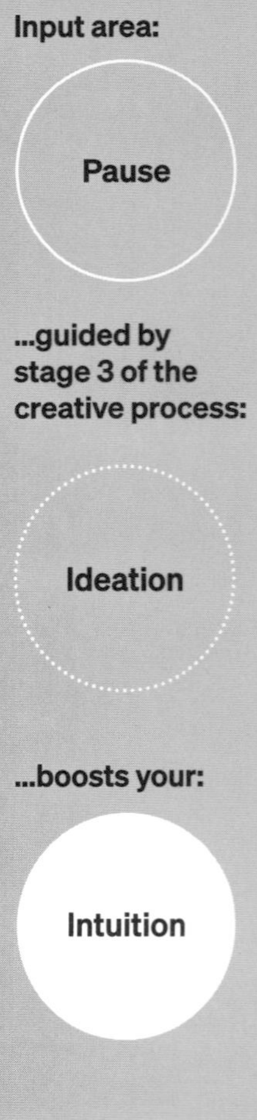

SELF-KINDNESS
SOLITUDE
NATURE
SPIRIT
WISDOM

How pausing reveals our intuition

I used to regularly feel like I was spreading myself too thin. There were times I looked at my to-do list in the morning and burst into tears.

I still feel overwhelmed at times. But since my burnout, I've built in habits and practices to support myself in the fast spinning pace of life.

The most powerful tool I have is a simple one: I don't turn my phone on first thing in the morning. I take the time to wake up to the day with myself first – I do some yoga and drink a cup of coffee whilst journalling. Only once my partner and I have had breakfast together do I switch my phone on and let the world in. There's a flow of text messages. An urgent email from a client. Adverts. Bold news headlines about an earthquake, and the latest political disaster. My attention is pulled away from the here and now, and scattered in every direction.

Thankfully I'm prepared for it, because I have given myself time first. I've already had a chance to listen to how I'm feeling and to figure out what I need from the day.

Every day can start with clarity and calm. Try it! Even if you wait to switch your phone on right after you're out of bed and your teeth are brushed. The important thing is to create this small space, before the day starts, to listen to your inner voice and emotions. You'll begin your day feeling like you matter – and by listening to yourself, you'll get to know yourself a little better.

Pausing can take many forms. It can be a phone-free morning, a year-long sabbatical, a weekend getaway. It can be a Friday afternoon off work, a lunch break away from your desk, a moment to pet your cat or gaze at the horizon. These big and small moments are opportunities for reflection, for the buzz and whirr of urgency to quiet so we can hear ourselves feel and think.

Pause to give space for the most important conversation of them all – with yourself. It's in moments of calm when things fall into place and you can **connect to your intuition**.

When you don't stop to pause...

...it's easy to miss what your inner self is trying to tell you. And when you don't take the time to listen to yourself, it's difficult to be sure of your feelings and emotions. Things might feel uncertain and unresolved.

Signs you're not pausing:

You are easily frustrated, irritated and overwhelmed.

You sense a disconnection from yourself, as if you've ignored an inner truth.

You find it hard to trust yourself and you dismiss your dreams and aspirations.

You see situations as either/or, without the nuances and grey areas.

Guided by the creative process: **Ideation**

To help you tune into your inner wisdom we're going to step into the third stage of the creative process: Ideation.

The Ideation stage is an opportunity to explore possibilities and dream up solutions. We're looking for new viewpoints and fresh ways of doing things. The goal is to come up with as many ideas as possible without filtering them – we can refine them later on.

There are a few ways us creatives generate ideas – brainstorming, mind mapping, sketching, storyboarding. I often think of it like putting two puzzle pieces together: they might be two completely different topics and meanings, but somehow when you slot them together a whole new picture – or idea – emerges.

Creative ideas aren't typically the product of rigid logic or overthinking. Their source is something more instinctive and intuitive. We all know the cliché of the best ideas appearing when we're not looking for them, usually in the shower, or perhaps while out for a walk. There's science behind this: research shows that doing something moderately engaging allows the mind to wander, which results in more creative ideas.[19]

A good idea can feel magical. We can rationalise the creative process all we like, but the sparky arrival of a brilliant solution – my own, or others' – still gives me a jolt of surprise and delight.

> When we pause, we can catch ideas that our intuition guides us towards.

There's a creative spirit swirling inside all of us. By pausing, and listening, we can tap into our intuition – and feel the ideas flow.

On the right are my early poster sketches for my talk at The Typographic Circle, London. I'm freely exploring letterforms and discovering new ideas along the way.

emmi
Emmi
EMMI
I'MME
EMMI

Pause within

Have you considered the possibility that you could have a little more time, but you've chosen not to? Perhaps you just can't help reaching for your phone first thing in the morning. Maybe you're wrapped up in work, or lose hours scrolling on social media. Society teaches us that 'busy' means 'successful', that grinding is good. It doesn't teach us the value of taking a break.

Resting gives us a chance to recharge, reconnect with ourselves, and show up fully. It can even help us come up with solutions for life's challenges. I think we all know this – so what's stopping us from taking a break?

In many cultures we are taught to prioritise everything but rest. It's hard to put our endless tasks on hold 'just' to have a moment to ourselves. In a culture and economic system that demands our productivity, it's no wonder we have forgotten that we all deserve the rest we need.

At first, it may feel difficult to shed the feeling that rest is indulgent. So, as you build more rest into your day-to-day life, it may be helpful to consider that pausing is, in fact, productive. Research shows that creative thinking is associated with more engagement with idle, free-flowing thoughts in restful states.[20] Not only are we more creative after taking a break, we have also stocked up on energy and improved our wellbeing.[21]

When I'm really in the midst of it, feeling like a squeezed piece of sour lemon, with overlapping deadlines, family needs, and heck, I'm sure I'm coming down with something... this is when it's most important to pause. Don't skip what might seem the easiest thing to let go of – it's actually the most important to hold on to. Take a literal breath. Give yourself time.

When you prioritise a pause for yourself, you create space – and everything shifts.

Sam Horner
Head of Apps UX
Google Play
USA

Creatives often thrive within established boundaries, yet falter when facing daunting deadlines or intense deep work. In these crucial moments, I urge my team to pause, breathe, and reconnect with their creative essence.

Identify the activity that revitalises you, that re-energises your creative flow. Perhaps it's a run, painting, or losing yourself in a video game. This isn't wasted time, but rather a strategic investment in maximising your creative potential.

FIVE STEPS TO REIMAGINING YOUR TO-DO LIST

1.
Jot down your full to-do list for the day. For each task, note how much time you expect it to take and how it makes you feel – joyful, purposeful, productive, or drained. Include taking breaks.

2.
Pick three tasks that feel purposeful - that feel important to your progress and align with your goals or values. Put a star by them: these will be your priority.

3.
For any tasks that feel draining or overwhelming, ask yourself: "Can I break this into smaller steps? Can I reframe it to feel more meaningful?" Even starting small can bring unexpected satisfaction.

4.
Review your list and pick 1-3 tasks that you can postpone, delegate, or say no to.

5.
Notice how you feel during your tasks and breaks. Note down your thoughts about what energises or drains you. Spotting these patterns can guide your future planning.

- [ ]
- [ ]
- [ ]
- [ ]
- [ ]
- [ ]
- [ ]
- [ ]
- [ ]
- [ ]

Mind your time

Imagine having enough time to do everything you want to do – write, draw, exercise, sleep in, do nothing at all – and never be short on time. Hard to imagine, right? But there's a term for what this would feel like: 'time affluence'. Unsurprisingly, 80% of employed US adults experience the opposite: 'time poverty'.[22] Although there's a practical reality behind both time affluence and time poverty, there are also ways in which thinking differently can alter our perception of the time available to us. It's possible to feel more time rich, without magicking up a 25-hour day.

The trick is to be disciplined about how we spend the time available to us. Are you putting it towards the people and activities that matter most to you? The exercise on the previous page will give you some clues as to how you're spending your time, and what you're prioritising.

If you already did the exercise, I want to ask you this: did your priorities include time for yourself? When we prioritise time for ourselves we experience something extraordinary: we have more time.

I do this by booking in what I call an 'Emmi Day' once every couple of months – a few hours to do anything I want to do. I've gone to an exhibition followed by lunch and a good book shop. I've stocked the fridge with my favourite foods and just pottered around the house. I simply do whatever I wish for an afternoon, on my own. Book a day like this in your calendar. Do it now. You can call it by your name, of course, or whatever you want! What matters is that the time is your own.

Harvard Business School professor Ashley V. Whillans recommends other ways we can avoid the constant feeling of being rushed. Her research has revealed that people who feel 'time rich' make small, simple decisions every day: they prioritise time over money, and outsource their most dreaded tasks to others. These choices unfortunately aren't affordable for everyone, but something else that the 'time rich' do – that costs nothing – is to actively savour the small moments in their daily life.[23] They take time over eating a meal and appreciate the beauty of a natural landscape or the changing sky.

By recognising just how fleeting the present moment is, we notice it more – and find a richness that has nothing to do with money.

DESIGN A SOLO DAY

Write down five things you will do on your own to make your day special. Next to each one, write down how you think it will make you feel.

Now, pick a date in your calendar and book it in.

AFTER YOUR SOLO DAY
Reflect on the experience. Were there any thoughts or insights that came to you during your solo day? Are you feeling different about any aspect of your work or life?

STEFAN SAGMEISTER

Graphic Designer, Storyteller & Typographer

SEVENTH YEAR SABBATICALS

Whenever I think about how useful it is to take a step back, I think of Stefan Sagmeister. He's a NYC-based Austrian designer and provocateur who has taken four (four!) year-long sabbaticals with the specific intention to recharge his creativity. Known for pushing the boundaries of graphic design through typography, installations and exhibitions, Stefan's fearless approach demonstrates how stepping away can lead to bold, boundary-breaking work. I was fortunate to catch him at the start of his latest sabbatical.

Having taken long pauses to recalibrate your inner compass, what has been the most surprising or transformative direction it has pointed you towards?

It has turned out that most of the projects I'm now glad we've done – the work I find meaningful – have had their origins in the sabbaticals. Without those pauses, almost all of what I consider the best work might never have seen the light of day. I also learned a lot about things I thought I'd like to do but, once I had the chance to try them, turned out to interest me less than I'd expected.

Do you see sabbaticals as a form of disruption – like the Ideation stage of the creative process, where you break routine to discover new perspectives and approaches?

Yes, disruptions of my own routines are important. I value these routines as they're often what make creating efficiently possible. But they also have a tendency to take over and push out new developments, which can feel scarier to try. They don't offer the comfort of what's already tried and proven. It also turned out that you can have different ideas when you have a year to think about them than when you only have a weekend.

You've taken three year-long sabbaticals so far. The first focused on thinking, the next on doing, and the last a mix of both. What's next?

I'm at the beginning of my fourth sabbatical now, and it's different once again. Because of the experience gained in the previous three sabbaticals, I've been able to transform my regular work into 'sabbatical work' – we no longer produce commercial projects in my design studio and focus only on projects I truly want to do.

In some ways, this sabbatical feels like a sabbatical from my sabbatical, as I'm still pursuing similar long-term thinking goals. The change is less dramatic, but I'm spending the year in three fascinating cities I don't know well: Madrid in Spain, Guadalajara in Mexico and Buenos Aires in Argentina.

1

2

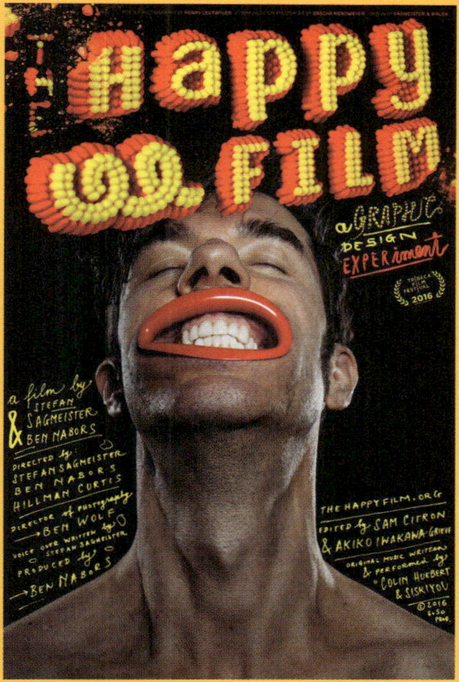

3

4

5

1 Beautiful Numbers
Stefan's process

2 Beautiful Numbers

3 The Happy Film

4 Things I Have Learned
in My Life So Far

5 Now Is Better

Seek silence

My worst guilty pleasure used to be binge watching TV series. Countless episodes would consume me for hours every day. I didn't like the fact but there seemed to be nothing I could do to change it. Until one summer in the Finnish Archipelago I forgot to bring my mobile wifi along. Almost immediately, I felt more present and relaxed. And I easily came up with all sorts of ideas for how to spend my time instead.

Back home in London, my life is full of noise: cars stuck in traffic, a blaring stereo, ambulance sirens, people yelling. One year, after my annual month in the Finnish forest, I had returned to the familiar playlist of urban commotion. The same night, I picked up a series I had been in the middle of watching before my trip. I realised I was doing it to find an escape. It was the only way I was able to find calm, to have one channel of noise I could fully focus on. This small realisation had a big impact on me. I could see how my constant need for distraction from the chaos meant that I never really heard myself.

I wanted to learn more, so I set about researching. I discovered a study that shows noise pollution causes hypertension, increases stress and is linked to heart disease, amongst many other negative impacts.[24] Scary stuff.

I had to ask: in a clanging, booming city like London, where can we find silence – even for a moment? I found the answer in the early hours, when the city was still asleep. I began to use earplugs for a couple of hours each day so I could hear my own thoughts, and listen to soundscapes that drowned out the city's noise. When I can, I venture into peaceful places like libraries, galleries and spiritual centres.

You might find silence uncomfortable at first. Many do. It can feel vast, and that's scary. What should we do with it? Where will it take us? I don't know the answer, but you do – because the quiet will lead you right back to your intuition.

<u>Lila Hamilton</u>
Designer & Art Director
Ireland/UK

Joy comes in glimpses and flashes – not so much a full thirst quenching glass, but small sips that are easily missed if you're not looking. Like the steam rolling off hot coffee, long rambling conversations with friends, softish warmish breezes, growing tomatoes from nothing, or a particularly good hug.

I realised that actually I found it most often in the pauses and in between places, and that sometimes I felt guilty for doing 'nothing'. There are such negative connotations around being idle and so much pressure to be productive. But working in sustainability it's becoming more and more clear that stopping, pausing, not producing or consuming might actually be the most helpful thing I can do. Not to mention the most delightful.

SILENCE SPOTTING

Silence is more than just the absence of noise. Use these four practices to embrace stillness as an active experience.

BREAKS

Sit still for 5-10 minutes and notice the subtle sounds around you (a passing car, the hum of the fridge), and focus on the silence between them.

BREATHING

Try to match your breathing with the silence. Inhale while listening to a sound, and exhale into the silence that follows.

Extend the silence on your exhale by holding for a moment before the next inhale.

REFLECTIONS

Spend five minutes in silence, then write down your reflections on how the 'sound of silence' felt - the moments of absence and their weight or lightness.

FOCUS

Pick an object to observe and sit quietly. Each time you hear a sound, use it as a prompt to return your attention to the stillness of the object.

The visual focus will support your listening, and help you stay present.

Tune in

I've talked about a few reasons why it's important we find calm, and how to do it. In the introduction chapter I shared what happened to me when I really, truly, stopped for the first time. I heard my inner voice enquiring how I'm doing. And I heard my own answer for the first time: I wasn't supporting my wellbeing in the ways I needed to.

When I finally heard this inner dialogue, I set out to improve my decisions, set healthier boundaries, learn to let go, and embrace the resources I already have. And ultimately, I developed the Creative Ecosystem model.

These were good things; but there's a catch. Connecting with ourselves can also mean connecting with difficult, unresolved emotions that can be heavy and hard to comprehend. For some people, tuning in like this can bring up traumas. It is helpful to talk about them with a supportive friend, a relative or a trained professional.

Coming face to face with our past traumas is a powerful thing. Ignoring these experiences doesn't make them disappear. Burying them can distort our view of ourselves and the world – which can impact the decisions we make, or make us feel unworthy.

Healing from trauma can be a lifelong journey, but it's a journey that can lead us back to our own creativity. The more in touch we are with our feelings, the better we are able to express them. We become kinder to ourselves, and therefore others. We find it easier to love ourselves, and therefore those around us. We feel closer to our creative self, and therefore our creative output.

Rebecca Porteous
Embodied Trauma Therapist
UK

We experience everything, including what's going on in our minds, through our bodies. By deepening your understanding of how your autonomic nervous system responds to both soothing and threatening stimuli, you can build a more connected and coherent relationship with your body and mind. This includes noticing how your body holds and processes what happens to you. It also means recognising that you might have more choice about that.

This process involves becoming more attentive and intimate with your 'felt sense' and finding safe, manageable ways to stay with uncomfortable feelings and sensations. While the instinct is often to move away from these feelings, you can learn, and eventually trust, that your body is capable of processing the charge they carry.

TUNE INTO YOUR BODY

Sit or lie down comfortably.
Take a slow breath.

1.
Ask yourself:
"What's the strongest sensation
I notice in my body right now?"

2.
Ask yourself:
"Where do I feel it? Is it warm, cool,
tight, expansive, still, or moving?"
Just notice, no need to change anything.

3.
If it feels good, rest in it. If it's
uncomfortable, gently move attention
between this and a neutral or pleasant
sensation (maybe your hands or breath).

4.
Notice any changes in your body
or shifts in how you feel.
Sensations often shift when
met with gentle attention.

5.
Place a hand on a soothing spot,
perhaps your heart, and take a few
breaths. Trust that your body is
capable of moving through experiences.

Pause with tools

At the cold, quiet turn of each yearly cycle, I get out my moss green ink pen and a special (work-free) sketchbook. I sit quietly, and think about what I want from the year ahead. I don't set goals or plan next steps; rather, I allow myself to dream. Where do I long to travel to? Who do I want to create with? What is a story I'm hoping to tell?

I approach it as if I'm in the Ideation stage of the creative process, letting my thinking free-flow, while connecting dots. I remind myself of my current 'brief', which is to answer the question: "What if I could do anything I want this year?" (See page 29 for a reminder of how to create your own personal brief).

This ritual at the beginning of each year is one of the tools I use to pause. That act of slowing down can take many shapes – a tea break, a long walk, a holiday. It's important to take rest that is unguided, that gives us a chance to 'switch off'. But it's also valuable to build in active, structured pauses that create an opportunity to dive deliberately into our inner world.

In the rest of this chapter, I'll share some of the tools I use to pause actively so I can strengthen not only my sense of intuition, but my whole Creative Ecosystem. My experience is that the very structure these tools create somehow opens up more space, more freedom to explore. They also make it easier to *actually do it* – which, in the frenetic midst of day-to-day life, can feel like the biggest challenge of all.

Prof. Holger Jacobs
Faculty of Design
HSD Düsseldorf
Germany

I'm not a big believer in the so called work-life balance. As creatives, we constantly observe, reflect and absorb inspiration from everywhere, blurring the line between work and life.

This makes it crucial to pay attention to where our input comes from. Are the ingredients for our creative output raw, fresh and individual, or predigested and processed by algorithms?

Like saturated fats, such overstimulation clogs our minds, driving us into cycles of indulgence and diet breaks, leading to stress and predictable outcomes. Never search for ideas – let them find you, and let them come from the real world.

ELEMENTS
Awareness Exercise

ETHER

This simple tool by Dr. Judson Brewer, a psychiatrist and mindfulness expert, is perfect to use at the start of any active pause. It brings several of your senses together at the same time, helping to ease anxiety and bring you into the present moment. It creates a sense of space and calm, which is what the element of Ether represents.

Hold up one hand with fingers spread apart and use the index finger of your other hand to trace its outline.

As you trace up a finger, inhale deeply. As you trace down a finger, exhale slowly.

Continue tracing your hand's outline, aligning your breathing with the motion.

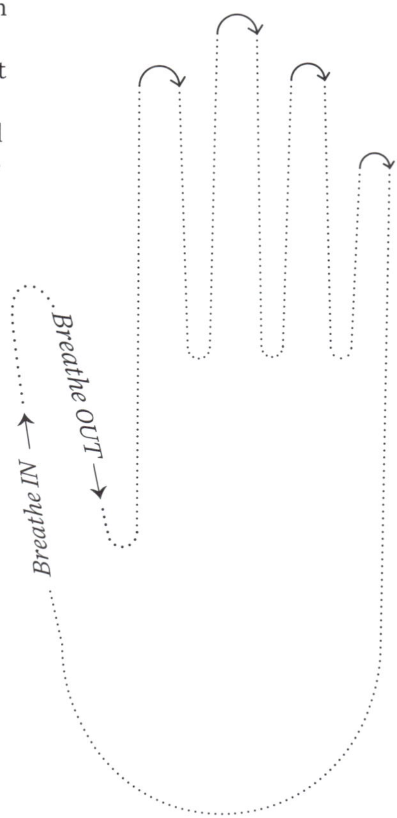

Create space

I've been on a life-long journey to find and afford a space that could be my creative sanctuary. I imagine it as a big open room, with high ceilings and huge windows with plenty of daylight streaming in. I would have a table for making, with all my tools handy, and another with my computer for screen-based work.

For the time being, I'm very happy with my current, humble, creative home. I've added small details to make sure my space gives me what I need, whatever my mood – a pinboard of fun visuals for when I need inspiration; a speaker for loud music when I need energy; an armchair by the window when I want to feel calm. Sometimes I want to *do* (sketch, research, dance), and other times I want to *be* (daydream, look at the horizon). The objects in my space help me do both.

For many of us, having lots of space for creativity feels like an impossible luxury. Still, there are small ways to be intentional about any space, however cramped. Removing clutter can be as important as adding details that support us. And even a small, affordable addition can change how a space feels. When I worked as a creative director, there wasn't much I could change about my team's space, but we could add plants. I took everyone to the garden centre, so we could see something grow when we sat down each morning, and a calming distraction from our screens.

Behavioural science shows that changing what we see around us can shape our actions – known as 'choice architecture' or 'nudge' interventions.[25] I want to draw more, so I have my pencils out in a cute tin pot. I'd like to build a gratitude habit, so I have a small notebook by my mousemat to write three lines in every day. I have playlists for different types of workflow – soundscapes for focus, upbeat rhythms for manual tasks.

Listen to your creative self. What does it need to flourish? Decluttering and organisation? Different lighting? Room to get messy? Honouring what it tells you will give it confidence and room to grow.

Dee Vallabh
Design Director
Fiji/New Zealand/UK

My environment greatly impacts how I feel, so I surround myself with things that make me happy. Books, prints, plants and knickknacks are dotted around my home and workspace, bringing me little pockets of joy. These personal, tangible and carefully curated treasures, each have their own story attached. I look to these with a sense of comfort, calmness and contentment.

With a toddler around, I've noticed her wooden blocks inspire colours, her scribbles evoke spontaneity, and her toys highlight the importance of tactility. These objects form an evolving collection, reminding me of who I am and what inspires me creatively.

CREATIVE SANCTUARY

Sit in your creative space, and experience it through all your senses. What do you see, hear, touch, smell? How does this make you feel?

Now sketch a floorplan of your ideal space. What sights, sounds, textures and scents would you like it to include? How could different parts of the space support your different creative needs - like inspiration, comfort, energy, calm?

SIGHT	SOUND	TOUCH	SCENT

Build rituals

The soul of my creative space is my record player. Whenever I need an energy boost, I pull a record out of its sleeve, gently lower the needle onto the groove, and listen to the warm crackle before the music begins. These familiar steps bring me a joyful kind of comfort – but there's more to it than that.

Playing music in this analogue, physical format means I hold the music in my hands. If I don't get up once side A finishes, that crackling turns into an unpleasant screech. So I get up, and flip it. Side B is soon over, and again I must get up. This pattern turns my listening into active listening: I'm repeatedly reminded of what it is that I'm doing. I am here, now, listening to this music.

The rhythm of my behaviour keeps my attention on the music. It's the same for our creativity: our rhythms of behaviour can help us tune in to our creative energy.

This is true even of our everyday routines. I start my day by organising my desk, getting my tools out and lighting some incense. These actions signal a new beginning, and honour what I need to kickstart my creative process for the day.

In this sense, we can think of simple routines as being rituals – deliberate, sacred practices that bring us into the present moment and signal something meaningful to us. They can guide our moods, helping us lean into a feeling of quiet or ride a jolt of energy. And when distractions creep in, rituals can help us refocus. They can help us work with our natural rhythms, and course correct when we want to.

Which daily rituals help sustain your creative practice? Everyday routines reframed as rituals can deepen your connection with your creative self. And, through repetition, they create consistency – which in turn helps us focus, and reminds us of our commitment to our own creative practice.

Kibir La Amlak
Music Producer & Performer
UK

It could be said that the boundary between ritual and the creative act has no clear start or end, yet arguably, both are empty acts without the presence of the other.

I endeavour to take no ownership over the source of my creative works, and ritual is the way I enact this intention – proclaiming to forces greater than myself that I am open to their mercy.

In fact, if I don't do this before a performance, I am overrun with anxiety. Making the creative act both an offering and an act of service allows me to trust what comes through me in a way that I could never trust myself. It forces me to pay attention to the music, as I have imbued its ownership with the highest authority of the universe.

EVENING ROUTINE	MORNING REFLECTION
EVENING ROUTINE	MORNING REFLECTION

SLEEP RITUALS

EVENING ROUTINES
Experiment with different ways to relax before bed, and log them using the 'evening routine' column on the left.

You could declutter your bedroom, adjust the lighting, or use essential oils. Try turning off screens for at least an hour before bed, and reading, journalling, or listening to music instead.

MORNING REFLECTIONS
The morning after each sleep time routine, log your results using the 'morning reflections' column on the right. Ask yourself:

How do I feel?
How restful was my sleep?
How long did I sleep?
Was it easier or harder to wake up?
Did the evening routine help me fall asleep more easily?
Did anything disrupt my sleep?

What small habit has had a big positive influence on you?

Making the deliberate choice to change, add or stop habits can have a profound impact on how we feel each day. In my Creative Wellbeing Insights survey, I asked creatives: what small habit has had a big positive influence on you?[26] Their answers revealed a truth that lies at the heart of the Creative Ecosystem model: **tiny, consistent habits can carve out pathways for better creative wellbeing.**

Reflecting

"In morning writing, answering the two questions 'what do I need *for* myself today?' and 'what do I need *from* myself today?'."

"Thinking about what is really important in life, changing perspectives."

"Stopping or slowing down when I notice I get wound up in something. Getting aware of my thinking and watching my thoughts from a neutral point."

Order of things

"Going to bed earlier."

"Walking. Before doing anything."

"Coffee AFTER water. Two litres a day minimum of water."

"Waking up at 5:30am."

Connections

"Talking to family."

"Getting some direct sun everyday for a few minutes in my face and, of course, therapy."

"Taking notice of what's around me, like clouds. I look up, people watch."

"Calling people when I miss them."

WHAT'S THE SMALL HABIT THAT HAS A BIG IMPACT ON YOUR LIFE?

No more

"Stopping myself from working or thinking about problem solving beyond the work hours I've outlined for myself."

"Saying 'No' more."

"Quitting coffee, I feel more stable without it."

Movement

"Walking home instead of taking the train."

"Swimming twice a week."

"Playing football weekly is a total break from everything."

"Little exercise breaks during the day."

Sunset and sunrise

"Morning drawing practice. I saw that I was improving after about six months."

"Moving my alarm clock away from the bed so I need to get up to turn it off. No more snoozing, and being groggy all day."

"Lighting up incense before going to sleep. It calms me down and allows me to have softer dreams."

Connect with nature

It took me a long time to write this book, and even longer to get started. When I finally began, I was sitting under an olive tree in a friend's garden. Back in London a few days later, I just couldn't get into it, despite my best intentions. A year went by before I began writing again, and this time the words flowed easily. Pages filled up fast.

What had changed? I was in nature again.

I finally realised that, for me to hear the words I want to share, I need to feel the natural world nearby. I had underestimated how important this was. As you read, know that every page was crafted with a tree, a boulder, or the sea in sight.

Perhaps it's because I want you to step into my inner world. And that inner world is one that was formed during my childhood in the forest – amidst pine trees and moss and sunlight and soil.

When I'm in nature, I can connect with my spirit. We all have our own ways to do that, but for me, the easiest way is to be alone in the wilderness. Finnish culture still retains some of our ancestors' beliefs – that humans are caretakers of nature, rather than rulers of it. During Midsummer, most Finns disappear from work into remote cabins to mark the longest day of the year (around 48% of the population frequently uses a holiday home – which are typically a basic dwelling with no running water).[27, 28] My brother shares his way of connecting to the wild in the quote on the right. Overleaf, you can read how it has shaped my sister Elsa and her unique Creative Ecosystem.

This relationship to nature is, of course, not unique to us Finns. We all benefit from time in the natural world. Even just looking at images of nature helps us recover from stress and improves our wellbeing.[29, 30]

Jere Salonen
Full Stack Web Developer
Finland

Once a year I spend a few weeks in Lapland, after hiking to a remote location for a day or three. Being in the wilderness has a profound effect on me.

At first, I worry about everyday concerns, but after a few days, my mind quiets, and I focus solely on the present. By the end, my thoughts return, but in a new, more meaningful order.

Nature reminds me that everything, including our projects and daily worries, is temporary. This perspective takes away stress and shifts my focus to the lasting impact of my actions.

Nature isn't just a backdrop – it's a force that connects me deeply to myself and the world. I hope everyone finds something in life that brings them this clarity and inspiration.

Right: Finnmark, Norway by Jere Salonen

ELSA SALONEN
Fine Artist

DISTILLING THE LIFE ENERGY

No one captures what it feels like to connect to the forest quite like my sister, Berlin-based fine artist Elsa Salonen. She explores the universe through the artistic alchemy of natural materials, weaving a sense of wonder, reverence and belonging into every piece. Her work feels like a whispered conversation with nature itself, rooted in the spirit of Finnish nature worship.

What does nature mean to you and your creative practice?
I prepare pigments for my artworks by grinding raw materials, such as animal bones and seashells, and extracting colours from medicinal herbs, mushrooms and algae. Each material holds unique knowledge. I view pigments as collaborators whose individual 'experiences' define the artwork's conceptual message. Through self-collected materials, many themes connect to specific natural sites, while universal themes are addressed with unique materials – like meteorites – collected with the help of specialists.

I distill colours from flowers, leaving them pale and colourless. The technique reflects how most organisms, both plant and animal, lose their colours in death – flowers wither, bodies blanch. Thus, all colours in nature signal the presence of a living force.

What role do Finnish forests play in your work?
My studio is in Berlin, but I spend part of the year in the Turku Archipelago, where I collect the majority of the materials for my works. For the last two summers, I learned to recognise and collect sleep-inducing medicinal plants. I read a lot, especially about old Finnish animist traditions that understood nonhuman entities, such as stones or trees, as equal beings with their own kind of consciousness. Some of these traditions are still practised, for example, by addressing special trees as sacred.

How do alchemy and animism come together in your art?
My works are marked by the artistic interpretation of alchemy, which explores the universe through natural materials, and animism, especially the Finnish nature worship. What they have in common is the perception of all surrounding nature as living and sensing. Medieval alchemists studied natural materials, which they also used to make colours. Through the materials, they sought to understand the surrounding universe as well as the interconnectedness of everything in the cosmos and the individual's role among all others' and within oneself. One of the most important steps in alchemy was repeated distillation, which left the purest essence of the substance – and the alchemist – in the glass flask.

1
2

3
4

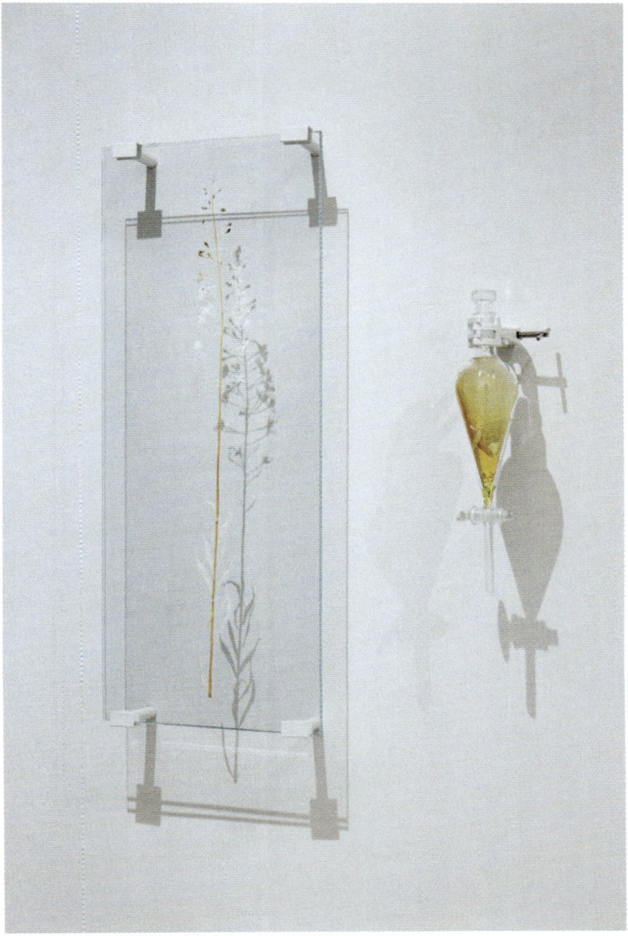

1 Elsa collecting the strong red-pigmented mushrooms Cortinarius semisanguineus from the Finnish forests

2 Harvesting Nymphaea leaves from the Finnish Archipelago shores

3 <u>Metsänpeitto</u>
Natural materials collected from the Finnish forests (painting: colour pigments extracted from alder barks, spruce cones, moss and mushrooms on glass, installation: swan feather, tops of three alder trees, lichen, whole and pulverised animal skulls, bones and teeth, powdered stones), salt, alum crystal, glass, metal 2021-2024, 215×175×415 cm

4 <u>Plants, Healers</u>: <u>Deep Sleep (Chamaenerion angustifolium I)</u>
Sleep-inducing medicinal plant rosebay willowherb collected from Finland, colour pigments and medicinal substances distilled from rosebay willowherb, isomalt, glass, metal 2023-2024, 60×25 cm (glass sheets)

04 MOVEMENT

Moving helps you sustain your output by strengthening your resilience.

Frame it like the *Development stage* of the creative process, and it will help your mind and body stay flexible.

Input area:

Movement

...guided by stage 4 of the creative process:

Development

...boosts your:

Resilience

ACCEPTANCE
REFRAME
FLOW
MOVE
ACCOMMODATE

How movement boosts resilience

We are in constant movement. The next project, the next idea, the next achievement; bereavement, falling in love, health worries. We are continuously evolving, only finished when we take our last breath. Until then, we're redesigning and refining. Life is a work in progress.

I happen to be writing this at the end of an incredibly challenging year. My family went through an unexpected and traumatising event, and we're in the process of trying to recover from the shock. Simultaneously, my partner and I rented an idyllic country cottage, where we can gaze at the sun as it rises from behind the mountains. We are dedicating half a year to our personal creative endeavours, and it has been soul enriching.

It's strange to experience this duality – such deep pain at the same time as such beauty. Somehow it's possible to feel awe and appreciation for life, even while finding it difficult to breathe.

Happiness and unhappiness are not, it turns out, opposite ends of a single spectrum. They operate on two separate systems within our psychology and biology. Negative and positive emotions arise in distinct ways, and are associated with separate brain structures and hormonal responses. While our fear response, for example, is concerned with responding to threats and leads to more pessimism and worry, our enjoyment system makes it possible for us to play and to grow.[31]

Navigating both positive and negative emotions – sometimes at the same time – is one of life's great challenges, but also a source of richness. When we experience the fullness of emotional complexity, we have the opportunity to expand a little – to grow, and heal. The key is to let thoughts and feelings come and go, whether they are pleasant or painful. By staying fluid in our mind and body, we can become more **mentally and physically resilient**.

When you lack movement...

... you might get stuck in negative patterns of thinking and find yourself ruminating on the same topic. Or you might be overconfident and miss opportunities to learn and grow. If you don't move your body, you're more likely to feel depressed, anxious and physically ill.[32,33]

Signs you're lacking movement:

You rigidly cling to your existing methods and resist new approaches.

You struggle to let go, holding on to ideas or situations that no longer serve you.

You avoid accountability and shift blame to others.

You become overly sensitive to discomfort, and give up easily to avoid challenges.

Remember: we all carry negative thoughts and emotions, and question our own capabilities. At times, getting physically active can feel especially hard. If your emotions ever feel too heavy to manage or start affecting your daily life, don't hesitate to seek support.

Guided by the creative process: **Development**

Strengthening your resilience is all about building your ability to adapt and recover. To explore this, we're going to draw on the mindset needed for step four of the creative process: Development.

The Development stage of a project is all about testing an idea we've come up with.

> We want to make sure the idea is resilient – that it really stands up. So we question it, poke it, stand back and reflect on it.

Importantly, we're not yet wedded to it. We're trying it on for size – we're open minded. We make mock-ups and dummies, and we ask for feedback. Sometimes we find that the idea is a flop, and that's fine. We move on, pick up a different idea, and do the same.

In the development stage, nothing is fixed. We test, explore and revise. We meet obstacles, but we know they're part of the creative process. Overcoming them pushes us further, and stumbling on them takes us in new directions.

Can you expand this approach to other areas of life? When we meet life's challenges with a development mindset, we're less likely to get stuck. With mental, emotional and physical flexibility, we can maintain and regain balance. Sometimes our only option is to accept the barriers that stand in our way – but this, too, calls for fluidity in our thinking.

On the right are my logo experiments for the design of the letter H. I've settled on a general direction - geometric shapes, lines - but there's still room to play. It's fun to experiment!

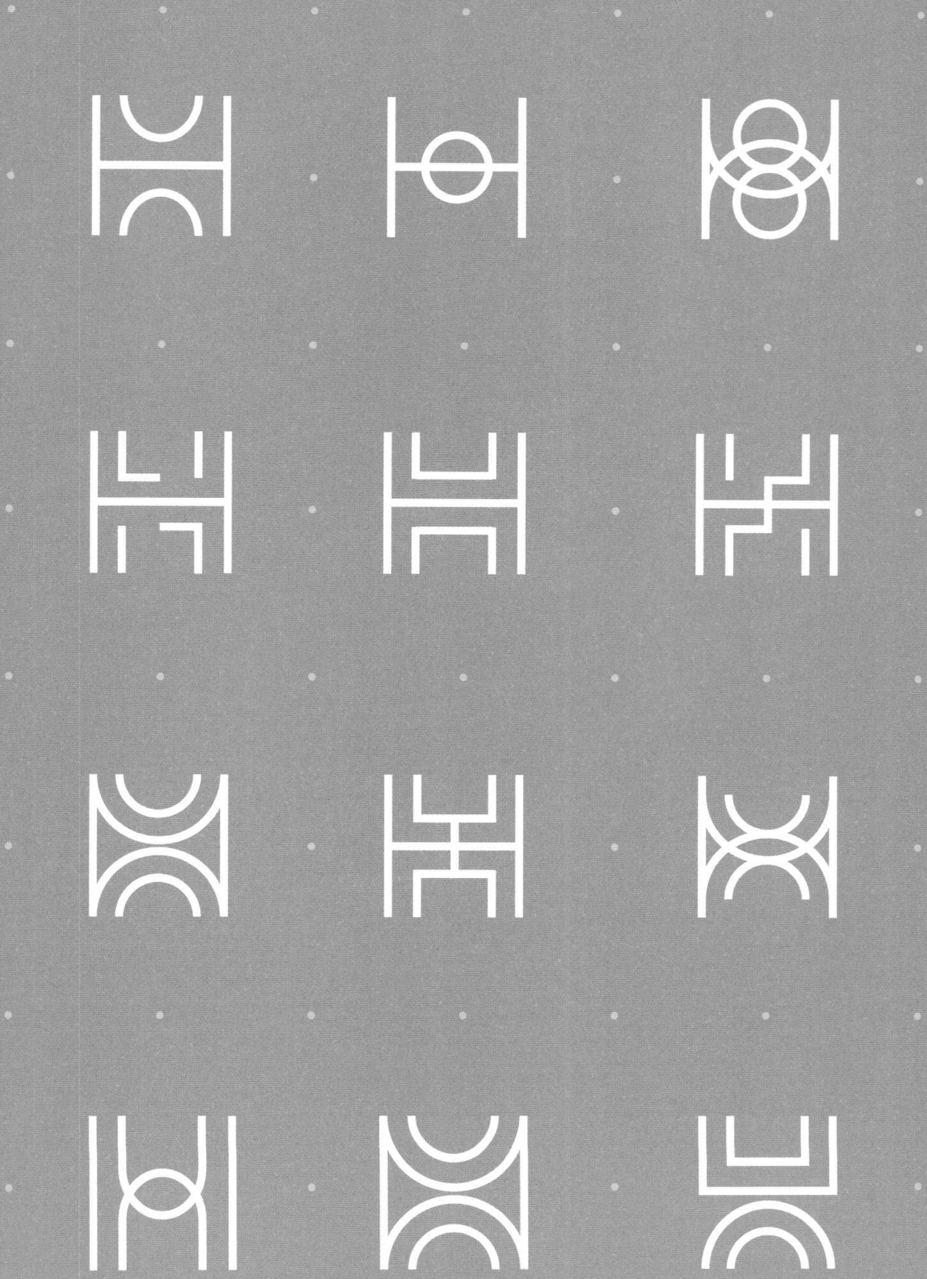

Move your mood

I used to be a ruminator. Thoughts and questions – even about minor, mundane things – would swirl endlessly: "Why did I say that? Why did I phrase it that way? I should have..." I had no real evidence that there was a problem, no sign that I'd upset anyone. But I was stuck in a loop of feeling that something was wrong.

One thing that helped me break out of my tendency to dwell was the discovery that we all tend to overestimate how deeply and how long future events will affect us emotionally, good or bad. One research study, for example, asked participants to compete for a romantic date. Participants predicted they would feel good if they were successful and bad if they weren't – but they overestimated how intensely they would feel these emotions.[34] These findings revealed to me the tricks my mind is playing, and that I'm bound to be exaggerating how badly I've messed up!

I also learned that our minds distort things in another way: negative experiences tend to impact us more than positive ones do. In a paper aptly titled 'Bad is stronger than good', researchers describe how we're quicker to form negative impressions than positive ones, and more resistant to change them. And we tend to overestimate the enduring impact of negative events more than we overestimate the effect of positive ones.[35]

Put this way, life sounds like an uphill battle. With our minds so ready to lead with the bad, how can we experience more of the good? My approach here is to do what I do when a creative idea isn't working. Rather than feel frustrated and give up, I try to look at it from a different perspective. We can do the same of any challenge. Ask yourself: are your bad feelings and stress caused by your life, or by your thinking?

The aim isn't to deny the challenges we face, but to find a balanced way to process them. Let unhelpful thoughts have their space, while you turn your attention to what matters.

Nicola Hamilton
President
Association of Registered Graphic Designers (RGD) Canada

Emotional turmoil is inevitable! If you imagine the process to be circular, the bit at the bottom will always be hard. It's the messy phase between a project's potential and its final execution. It's the part where hundreds of ideas litter the pasteboard and our job becomes sifting through them. Every idea feels like an extension of our being and judging them feels like a judgement against ourselves.

The trick is to become aware of this stage and accept it as unavoidable. The only way through the mess is to do the work. To put your head down and muscle through it. The more disciplined you become, the easier it will be to accept that the good stuff is coming.

REFRAME AND RESET

Turn a tired thought into a fresh perspective.

Based on Dr Aaron T. Beck's work on Cognitive Behavioural Therapy (CBT), later expanded by Dr David D. Burns.

1. Write down a negative thought. For example:

"I'm not creative at all."
An untrue label

"I'm not cut out for this."
All or nothing thinking

"I'm always a mess."
Sweeping statement

"I'll never come up with a good idea."
Worst case thinking

"Nothing I create is worth sharing."
Ignoring what works

"This project will probably flop."
Gloomy predictions

2. Challenge your thought. Ask yourself: "Is this 100% true? What evidence says otherwise?"*

3. Reframe it.

"Creativity comes in many forms, I just need to find mine."

"Not every project works, but it's part of the journey."

"Things feel messy sometimes, but I've made it work before."

"Creative blocks happen, but inspiration always returns."

"Some parts need improving, but there's plenty I've done well."

"I don't know the outcome, but I can focus on doing my best."

* Keep a folder, physical or digital, of positive moments. Collect kind messages, encouraging feedback and reminders of projects you're proud of. When self-doubt creeps in, revisit it to reconnect with what's gone well and how others have valued you and your work.

Do you have repeated negative thoughts about yourself?

A whopping 87% of the creatives taking part in my research survey struggle with feelings of inadequacy.[36]

Many shared their experiences of self-doubt, often fearing they were too slow, lacking creativity, or feeling out of touch.

"I'm not enough..."

"I'm not good enough and specifically not creative enough... or maybe just the wrong kind of creative."

"I often feel I'm not doing enough and that resting isn't a good enough use of my time."

"Not organised enough. I'm not focused or disciplined enough."

"I am not good at this, my artwork is awful, no one will ever buy it."

"Am I worth the money?"

"Oh that's not a clever idea."

"Don't let people know you don't know. You're falling behind."

"I am not a good enough designer or creative, usually in the form of 'what will people think' or 'there are people who could do this waayyy better than me'."

"My work isn't good enough, I am CRAP at communicating and making connections."

"I'm a starter and not a finisher."

"I'm too..."

"I am worried that I am too slow... I don't allow myself time to produce qualitative work."

"You are too lazy, you don't work hard enough, you repeat the same mistakes over and over again."

"There is a general theme around my age placing me outside of what is current (I'm over 50). This leads to self-doubt and job insecurities."

"What will they think...?"

"I worry about what other people I deem 'more creative' than me think of my work and creative choices."

"I keep thinking: 'I have to impress these people', 'should I go on and confront their ideas?', 'I don't feel I belong'."

"I have massive impostor syndrome, and all the negativity that goes along with that."

WHEN DO YOUR NEGATIVE THOUGHTS TEND TO SHOW UP?

Go with the flow

I don't think I have ever been more overwhelmed with excitement than when I got accepted to Fabrica, Benetton's communication research centre. There, in a striking building in the Italian countryside designed by renowned Japanese architect Tadao Ando, I would join some of the world's most interesting thinkers to be part of experimental creative projects. A month out of university, I simply could not believe my luck.

At first, I thought this was it – I had reached the kind of happiness that would stick. But, as always, life kept moving. The excitement faded, the newness wore off, and before I knew it I was back in my usual rhythm. I was grateful but not glowing, focusing on new goals and dreams. I was back at my baseline.

And then, as if to balance things out, life threw me a curveball: I broke my right elbow. Suddenly, the simplest things became complicated. Doing my work, tying my shoes, pouring a cup of tea, all had to be done differently (or not at all). At first, I was incredibly frustrated by how little I could do. Then slowly, I started to adapt. I found new ways of getting dressed, and even found the fun in learning to sketch with my left hand.

Happiness isn't a finish line or a perfect state we reach. It's a feeling that's in flux – and however far we're knocked off our normal emotional course, for good or bad, we tend to return to whatever 'usual' feels like for us. Psychologists call this 'Happiness Set Point', and it's determined largely by our genetics, personality and temperament.[37]

No matter how high or low life takes us, we tend to return to our baseline over time. The good times settle. The hard times pass. What matters isn't controlling every event but learning to ride the waves as they come.

Daniel Eatock
Artist & Designer
UK
When nothing seems to be working, I look at my cats – everything will be okay!

NEXT TIME A DIFFICULT EMOTION ARISES, TRY THIS

Based on Dr Russ Harris's 2009 work on Acceptance and Commitment Therapy (ACT).

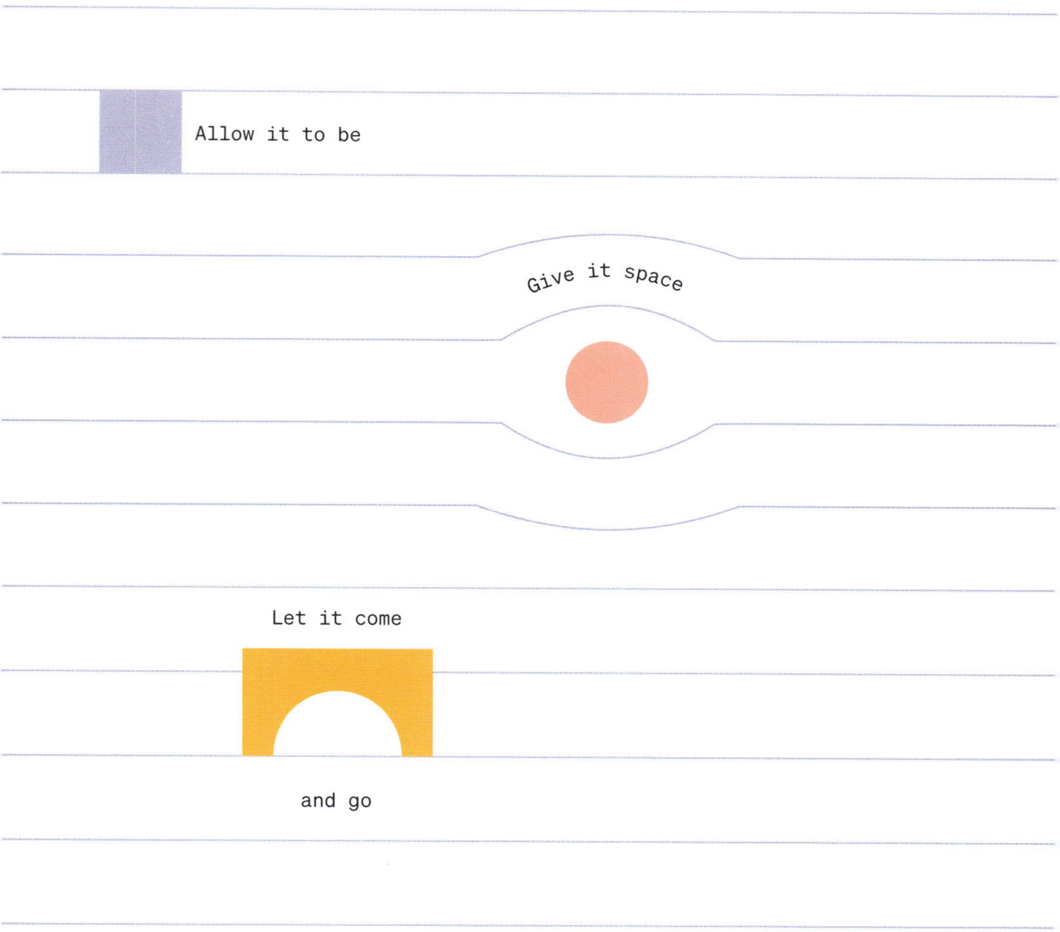

Allow it to be
Instead of pushing it away, acknowledge it's there.

Give it space
Name it: "This is fear" or "this is sadness". Naming helps create distance.

Let it come and go
Allow it to shift naturally.

Drop the struggle
Breathe with it. No need to fight, just let it move through you.

Shift perspective

One day at Fabrica I was struggling with a layout design for a film poster that was to be shown at the Venice Film Festival. I felt I'd tried everything, rearranging the elements on the page a hundred different ways. I was stuck.

It got late in the day and my creative director, Omar Vulpinari, noticed me struggling. "When you're stuck, play with scale", he said. It was exactly the advice I needed to hear. A shift in perspective set me in motion, and I was finished in an hour.

It's moments like this that remind us that challenging circumstances don't have the power we think they do to overshadow our emotional world. The situations we find ourselves in can feel all-consuming, but they don't always need to be. We often have the choice to change how we think or act, which soon changes how we feel. In fact, scientists studying happiness have found that just 10% of our happiness is determined by our circumstances. The practices and thought patterns we choose to engage in, on the other hand, account for 40% (and the rest is down to genetics).[38] We've got more control over our feelings than we give ourselves credit for.

From a new angle, a challenge can even reveal itself to be an opportunity. The experience of overwhelm, looked at another way, is a chance to focus on what matters most. Feeling envious of a colleague can give us clues to our real desires and goals. Even an argument with a friend – however bad it feels – can teach us how to communicate better, how to listen, how to adapt.

When I experienced burnout, the thought of creating was overwhelming. Instead of pushing creativity away, I got curious about my feelings of overwhelm. I looked more closely at the creative process itself – and found there the building blocks of what would become the Creative Ecosystem model.

Zipeng Zhu
Artist & Creative Director
Dazzle Studio
USA/China

Life is tough, super duper tough, but if you only focus on the difficult parts, they will only pile on top of each other and make everything more unbearable. In fact, comedy equals tragedy plus time; I can almost always find something funny or positive from something terrible.

Challenges aren't roadblocks; they're chances to rethink, reinvent, and push beyond limitations. As an artist, I believe the most authentic and exciting work comes from within; to embrace the uncomfortable is one of the more honest ways to create. The work should feel like an explosion of personality, a visual melody that moves people. The more I trust my own instincts and let my creativity shine, the more I discover that the world is as exuberant as I dare to make it.

THE FLIP-SIDE

Think of something that frustrated you recently, a big or small setback.

1. Write it down from your initial perspective. What felt hard about it?

2. Now reframe it, and rewrite what happened. In what ways was it an opportunity or a lesson?

Use humour

So far in this book, we've worked through the early stages of the creative process – Briefing, Research, Ideation, Development. We'll soon come onto the final stage, Creation. However different these stages might be, whichever of our talents and strengths they call on, most creatives have a companion every step of the way: creative self-doubt.

Self-doubt is the pesky voice that has you questioning your idea, comparing yourself to others and overthinking the details. I don't like this voice. Like an unwanted house guest, it refuses to take the hint and move along. Thankfully, I've discovered a repellant. If there's one thing that the doubting voice fears, it's being the butt of a joke.

When we look at a challenge head on, it feels anything but funny. It looms, and blocks our path. But if we find a way to look at it sideways and catch a glimpse of its absurdity – a tiny detail, an ironic twist, the way everything went wrong all at once – there's a chance we'll find something to laugh at.

One day at Fabrica, I had to share some work in progress with my colleagues on stage in the auditorium. As I walked up to the front, the doubting voice was having a field day ("You're not good enough! They won't like your idea!"). Then something unexpected happened: my fellows descended into a debate about the rightness or wrongness of my work. I suddenly saw the scene from outside myself: my audience's heads turning, as if at a tennis match, to watch the opinions hurled back and forth across the room; and me, silent at the front, watching. I giggled. And, lo and behold, the doubting voice was gone.

To be able to laugh at frustrations and even hardships isn't just a relief – it's resilience. Researchers have found that a good sense of humour can boost life satisfaction and help us cope better with difficult life events.[39] When we laugh more, we can do more.

Hjalti Karlsson & Jan Wilker
Co-Founders &
Chief Creatives
karlssonwilker inc.
USA

Apart from enjoying making each other laugh every day, humour also helps set the tone in the studio, encouraging everyone to be irreverent and unafraid to share their thoughts and ideas, however strange they might be.

Humour requires a certain playfulness, with words, shapes, and/or situations. This playfulness opens up a whole universe of design and communication possibilities that 'serious', dogmatic approaches would not allow for. And if something communicates with a certain lightness or unusual un-seriousness, it tends to become more accessible, prompting curiosity rather than 'high-threshold anxiety' or, even worse, boredom.

DOODLE AND MOVE

Doodle your problem as a monster. Add googly eyes or funny hats to see it as something you can play with, change or even laugh at.

JEAN JULLIEN
Visual Artist

FINDING A TWIST

I find so much wonderfully bendy thinking in French artist Jean Jullien's work. He reframes simple, everyday moments to feel sharp yet familiar – always with a dose of wit. And his integration of social and cultural themes into his work makes me feel seen, understood, part of the story. From illustration to furniture to spatial installations, his creative range is dynamic and ever expanding yet always recognisable as his.

Do you think humour has a special role in design and art?

I take a lot of inspiration from things that annoy me or make me tick. I try to find the funny side and turn it into comedy. I think humour is a great softener and very binding. But it's a tricky tool, especially in today's globalised culture. The internet enables us to share and communicate 24/7 everywhere, but we should remember that there are subtle cultural differences – comedy might not always be understood as intended. This doesn't mean you shouldn't share it, but you should understand it might backfire. As the saying goes, "You can laugh about everything, but not with everyone."

How do you deal with lack of motivation?

That doesn't seem to happen to be honest. I think I'm a 'reactive' creative. I react to what is around me or what I see. And I'd say the only thing I lack is time.

I've read you don't work digitally. How do you generate and refine ideas into meaningful visuals?

I work fast. I don't do much preparatory sketching, and favour impulsion. I see something, draw it, then move on. I trust my instinct and evaluate the result afterward. It's not necessarily the smartest way to work, but it's mine. As for digital, I love drawing on paper, then photographing and colouring it on the computer. So it's not that I don't work digitally at all but there's always a paper start.

How has your approach to creativity evolved over time?

I got tired of creating 'content' for social media. I wanted to explore other things and have more authorship in my work. At one point, I felt obligated to share content daily to stay relevant. I looked back and felt my work lacked substance, that it could all be deleted in a click, and I was just one of thousands making humour-based work to entertain people on their phones. I'm exaggerating a bit, but it felt that way. Doing more gallery shows and personal projects helped. I still love sharing online but try not to create specifically for that medium.

1 Then, There Jean's sketchbooks, photo by GNC Media

2 Paper Society, Publik Gasan
Photo by Serim Yang

3 The Cousins Chair, Case Studyo

4 Le Ratisseur, Filili Viridi
Jardin des Plantes, Ville de Nantes

5 NOUNOU

6 FRICOTE

1

2

3

4

5

6

Move your body

After my burnout, I did something I'd never done before: I started dance classes. It started slowly, with classes at the local community hall. Once I got going, and I felt my body and mind responding positively, I was hooked. I was soon travelling across London to find classes most days, and dancing for six hours every week. The more I danced, the more I felt my confidence and motivation blossom. I began to sleep better, feel stronger, think more clearly and have more ideas.

My experience is that physical activity – whether dancing, walking, jogging, yoga, swimming – is as much about moving our mood as it is about moving our body. Research has found that around half an hour of moderate intensity exercise lifts our mood, even among those suffering from depression.[40] Something as simple as walking can even boost our creativity.[41]

Try this by going for a walk, and see how your focus and emotions shift. If you keep the momentum going and move regularly, you'll be doing your future self a favour by protecting yourself from stress, depression and dementia, amongst a long list of health and wellbeing benefits.[42]

Being active is like unlocking a secret superpower. Its effects are both immediate and long term, which means it can help us feel better here and now, and in the future.

Nelly Ben Hayoun-Stépanian
Designer of Experiences, Filmmaker, Creative Director & Analog Astronaut
UK/Algeria/Armenia/France

Sport, boxing particularly, is both my escape and a driving force for creativity. I started learning how to box with the legendary Hector Roca aka 'Papa', who trained more than 20 world champions at Gleason's Gym – it ended up with me getting on with my first fight.

This was one of the most empowering experiences of my life. Boxing is a way of letting go of the pressures of the day and focusing totally on something else, whilst at the same time inspiring new ideas in my design practice. These days I am trained by head coach Natasha Patterson, an absolute force and inspiration to the community at Pedro Youth Club in Hackney and it is an honour to learn this craft with her.

ELEMENTS
Movement Exercise

WATER

Find enough space so you can extend your arms fully. Stand with your feet hip-width apart. Take a few deep breaths, relax your shoulders and imagine your body as a stream of water, ready to flow.

Slowly lift your arms above your head, then let them drift back down, as if waves are rolling in and out. Repeat, imagining waves rippling away from your fingertips.

Become still, then shift your weight side to side, letting your body gently sway like a stream flowing around pebbles. Keep your movements smooth and fluid.

Softly twist your torso, allowing your arms to follow, like water swirling in a whirlpool. Keep the motion continuous and steady.

Gradually slow your movements until you come to stillness. As your movements settle, imagine ripples of calm and clarity extending outward. Hold onto this openness and carry it with you into what comes next.

Voice it

I felt a tingling in my hands, and my chest was getting tighter. I was surrounded by 150 people, all gathered for the Annual General Meeting of a membership organisation I was working for. They had just been shown a redesign of their logo, and the reaction wasn't good. "I don't get it," I heard muttered. "Looks unfinished," someone else said quietly. "Bring back the old one!"

What they didn't know was that I, the designer, sat amongst them, and was about to walk up to the front to share the wider visual identity presentation. It was clear I was facing a tough audience. My body was tense, and I felt the telltale physical signs of anxiety – anger, even.

I had two choices: talk from a place of fear, or talk from a place of trust. And I trusted my design. I knew why the logo looked the way it did, why I had made the choices I had and, well, why it worked.

I wanted to speak with ease and confidence, so I knew I needed my body to be calm. I took a few deep breaths, and introduced my slide show. By the time I was finished, everyone was clapping. It was no standing ovation, but it was acceptance and understanding.

I'm accustomed to talking about my designs, and after close to three decades in the industry, it comes with ease. Still, when it comes to talking about my personal feelings and needs, I still feel the fear. And research suggests that suppressing our emotions is a bad idea, with major consequences for our overall health.[43]

Emerging science even suggests that simply using our vocal chords, in a meditative hum, is an effective way to reduce stress.[44] I sometimes feel a spontaneous hum coming on when I'm walking in the forest, and I always let it out – it makes an enjoyable walk feel even better.

Put self-consciousness aside, and humming is something that you can do almost anywhere – whilst washing up, working, or before presenting to a tough crowd. Focus on where you feel the vibrations in your body, and let your voice move you.

Evelyne Brink
Voice and Speaking Coach
Brink Coaching Ltd
UK

In the beginning was the sound – before we made sense, we made noise. And that noise is telling you something. My voice tells me how I'm feeling – now that's what it means to 'listen to yourself'!

Want to feel better? Use your voice. Set the intention to free yourself. Vocalise. You don't just make sound; you make space. Shake off stress, shift your state, surprise yourself. Your voice isn't just for communication. It's for calibration.

NAME IT

Explore your voice by connecting to an emotion and playing with expression.

1.
Say your name aloud using different tones and emotions: soft, loud, joyful, nervous or calm. Vary the volume, speed and rhythm. Notice how each feels in your body and affects your mood.

2.
Choose an emotion to explore: joy, anger, sadness or excitement. Express it with sounds, like hums, sighs, laughs or shouts. Let your breath and voice flow freely.

3.
Say your name out loud using different emotional tones: say it confidently, playfully or softly. Allow your voice to rise or fall to match the emotion you're expressing.

Up and move

After every dance class, without fail, I leave feeling lighter, more empowered, joyful. Even if I'd arrived feeling weighed down by the world, I soon find that moving to the music has connected me to the present moment, to my breath, to my body. The people around me, immersed in their own limb-flailing, help me feel the freedom to let go. I had been heavy; now I'm lifted up.

Movement doesn't have to mean strenuous exercise. Some days call for energy and speed, when we are feeling restless or raring to go – running, dancing, the gym. Other days we feel low or quiet, and need softness and kindness instead – yoga, a slow walk, sweeping the floor. Let your mood shape the way you move.

Simply going for a walk is a useful default option to keep your Creative Ecosystem resilient. Not least because researchers at Stanford University have found that walking can boost creative output by around 60%.[45]

There are days when motivation feels so distant it might as well be on another continent. On those days I make small movements, like stretching my arms or rolling my shoulders. Movements don't need to be big to be meaningful.

Similarly, when we are developing our creative ideas, sometimes just a small nudge makes everything fall smoothly into place. Other times, some heavier creative strokes are needed to get the idea working.

Shelaine Prince
Co-Artistic Director & Events Manager
Ignition Dance Company
Jamaica/UK

Whether it's a dance class, the gym, dancing alone at home, or socialising, just tap, bounce, nod, jiggle and jump. Give in to the rhythm of your heartbeat. We all receive music differently, and that's the beauty of movement.

Remind yourself of where you are in this moment – what can you smell, feel, and hear? Move with these senses. The more you allow yourself to move, the more your inhibitions will drop. Trust your body to move with love and let go. Remind yourself to LET GO. The rhythm of your own heartbeat will never lead you astray.

WAYS TO MOVE

List ideas for low, moderate and high-intensity 30-minute activities. Now book it in!

GENTLE like a walk or stretching.

ENERGISING like dancing or running.

POWERFUL like jumping jacks or skipping rope.

SHOJI YAMASAKI

Performance Artist & Choreographer

CHALLENGING CHOREOGRAPHIC NORMS

Experiencing Shoji Yamasaki's performance art feels like stepping into a deeply intimate and playfully unpredictable world. Somehow, the way he moves changes how I see everyday scenes. Shoji is a Japanese-American transdisciplinary creative based in the USA, whose site-responsive works explore community, space and time in a way that demonstrates just how powerful movement is for a dynamic, expansive creative practice.

You've described the world as choreographed on micro and macro levels. How does this perspective shape your creativity?

Dance is often defined by tradition and, often, Eurocentric vocabulary that is trained into human bodies. My current focus is to stray away from those vocabularies and direct our attention to the more natural movements that constantly surround us. The creation of life here on Earth and the gestural habits born out of living in myriad climatic environments – these are all sources of my inspiration. With that focus, we can ground and connect with nature, expand our connection to the entire universe, and be conscious of the impact we can create for future generations.

In your ongoing series, Littered MVMNTS, what goes through your mind as you observe and embody the motion of an object?

When I encounter moving trash, my immediate thought is where and how my limbs will be when I later embody it. Every piece of trash is unique and depends heavily on the weather that day – whether it's windy or not – and the location where the trash has ended up. It's interesting to see how trash has its own character – some are camera shy, some may just run away, and some will really 'dance' for you. The focus is on movement and form, leaving interpretation and emotional responses to the viewer.

What role does humour play in connecting with nature and the discarded objects you work with?

Humour doesn't play a role in my relationship with nature. Rather, I use humour as a connective tissue between discarded objects and the viewer through my embodiment of trash. In other words, I see myself as a medium between inanimate trash and animate viewers, where humour is born through the translation of such movement onto a human body. Humour is also an expression that people can connect with more easily than others. This allows a human connection that is born out of positivity, which in turn creates a positive impact when people are presented with litter in front of them – encouraging a cleaner community and, ultimately, a cleaner Earth.

Shoji Yamasaki emulates the movement of plastic bags and other debris caught in the breeze in his captivating choreography series Littered MVMNTS.

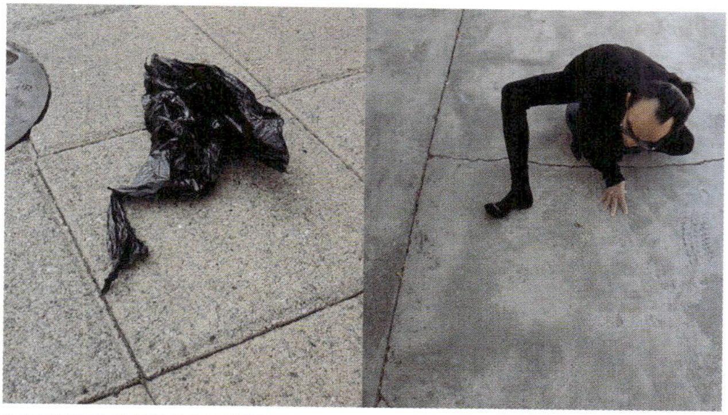

1 Black Bag Leg

2 Blue Oreo Wrapper

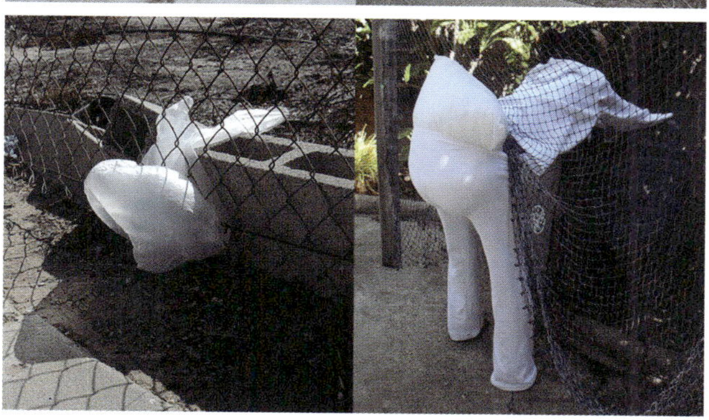

3 Trash Bag Booty

4 SunnyD Label

Be brave

Growing up, I hung out a lot with my cousin. We had the wildest plans. We were going to climb the highest tree, and dig a hole all the way to the other side of the world. I'm almost certain we had everything in place to time travel.

Surprisingly enough, our plans never came to fruition. But the six-year-old me had full confidence in our capabilities. Children have the extraordinary and useful ability to believe they can do more than is possible. This isn't just naivety – it's a valuable tool that pushes us to try, fail, and try again without being crushed by setbacks.

Most adults lose this boldness. We become more aware of failure, of our own limitations. What would happen if, when faced with resistance, we tapped into the courage we felt as a child?

All movement comes with resistance. Whether you're kicking against water while swimming, or lifting a heavy suitcase, the laws of physics mean we must push against an opposing force. That's how we build strength – our muscles depend on it.

Resistance might not be physical. I have a good few ideas for self-initiated projects I'd love to work on, but I can feel the fear and self-doubt pushing against me when I try to move forward.

Just like swimming against the current builds up our shoulder muscles, pushing back against mental resistance can make us stronger, more resilient.

We could all benefit from being more childlike, when it means being more brave. Just like children, we grow by trying things that feel just out of reach – and believing we're capable, even before we've proven it.

Guillermo Flores Pacheco
Art director, Illustrator & Designer
Mexico

I've realised how stubborn I can be in the face of change. I react negatively to it, and while it feels normal to resist, I don't realise that my reaction holds me back, keeps me stuck, and shuts me down. Then, when fear comes close to paralysing me, I take a step back and look at the bigger picture and put problems into perspective.

That's when I can see the obstacles in my way, accept them, and move forward. I can step into the unknown with confidence because I can finally see the way ahead.

On the other side of change, I find my voice again. Change isn't just a challenge – it's an opportunity to discover my strength.

ACTS OF COURAGE

If you were fearless, what three activities would you do? Next to each activity, write down how doing it would make you feel.

05
JOY

Feeling joy helps you sustain your output by giving you a source of energy.

Treat it like the *Creation stage* of the creative process, and it will help you find your spark.

Input area:

Joy

...guided by stage 5 of the creative process:

Creation

...boosts your:

Energy

HAPPINESS
FUN
GRATITUDE
SAVOURING
PLAY

How joy fuels energy

When I was stuck in work tunnel vision – with nothing but deadlines, to-do-lists and grind in mind – I failed to understand something that is universally true, yet all too easily overlooked. Namely, that the flame of creative energy doesn't burn brightly on its own. It needs fuelling.

But how, and what with? The beauty of it is that creativity, in its purest form, can actually feed itself. Let me explain.

Whatever form of creativity exists in your career and life, I doubt it found its way there through a task list. Our creative sparkle is at its shiniest when we've left the 'to do's behind, and are doing something we don't 'have' to do – having fun, experimenting, playing around with something new. The ideas start to bounce around, the possibilities feel exciting, something colourful or clever starts to take shape. Maybe we're having so much fun that we set out to make a profession out of it.

Over time that sparkle fades when creative work becomes routine. When our job requires a stream of creative outputs, we forget that there's a special value in creating things for the sheer fun of it. We don't have – or don't make – time for creativity that has no purpose or payment attached to it.

We have overlooked the fact that some of our creative endeavours take from us, while others give. Deadlined work projects come with client expectations and a heavy dose of obligation, all of which can douse the flame of our creative energy. Spontaneous creativity, on the other hand – the kind that is unpressured, free to spring in any direction we choose – is a source of joy that fans that all-important flame. We can find this joyful, self-sustaining creativity in small, everyday places: in baking cat-shaped cookies, or messing around with a ukulele, or organising stones by size.

These apparently meaningless moments have a profound power to feed our creative spirit. They help us glow, and that light can find its way into our daily commute, our work projects, our conversations with colleagues. Joy has that magical quality of lingering, so that each burst of fun radiates out into the rest of the day. The trick is to build more of this brightness into your days, so you can feel the **flame of your creativity** burn bright.

When you lack joy...

...things can feel flat and deflated, like you've lost your spark. You don't feel excited about doing things or have the energy to start. You might feel like there's an inner battle between your feelings of resistance, and your desire to do and make.

Signs you are lacking joy:

You feel empty and there's no excitement.

The expectation to produce something feels heavy and puts you off starting.

You avoid the unpredictable, messy moments where creativity often thrives.

The need to be perfect keeps you from ever getting started.

Guided by the creative process: **Creation**

To guide us on the journey back to joy, we are going to look at the final step of the creative process: Creation. It's at this stage that we bring our ideas to life.

In the preceding stages of the creative process we laid the groundwork, experimentally and tangibly. Now it's time for hands-on creation: writing, designing, building, coding, painting or crafting. It's a deeply immersive stage where our tools meet our ideas.

At its best, the Creation stage can feel electric. We feel our skills and our vision click together into place. We enter a flow state, where the work feels natural, effortless, and time seems to fade away.

> We know exactly what to do, without trying.
> We feel *alive*.

Turning an idea into something you can hold, hear or see can be deeply satisfying. This final step in the creative process validates all the efforts that went before – all the Research, Ideation and Development that led you to this point.

It can even become the jumping off point for new ideas, prompting us to explore new layers of expression and imagination. Joyful creativity is generative – it multiplies itself, and is a birthplace for abundance. In this sense, the final step of the creative process is not an end, but a beginning.

Studio Emmi turned 20 years old in 2025, and I had so much fun creating a set of stickers to celebrate the milestone by spreading a little positivity and design magic. To see them move and use them on Instagram or other apps, just type @StudioEmmi in the GIPHY sticker search.

STUDIO EMMI
20 YRS
POSITIVE CREATIVITY
SAY YES
LOVE
BORN TO
EST 2005
CREATE
20 CHEERS
PAPERCLIP DREAMS
DESIGN AND SHINE
TAKE A BREAK
ERASE DOUBTS

Inner joy

I've found my happy place. It's not a sandy beach, or a spa, or even the island in the Finnish archipelago I talk so much about. It's actually not a place at all: it's anywhere that I've got the time and space to play and create. I take my happy place with me – to the forest, where I photograph mosses up close; to the shoreline, where I scout for shells and corals to sketch; to my home studio, where I cut shapes out of coloured paper and get excited when the forms accidentally become complementary.

My happy place just calls for a window of time and a material to create with. There's no room for self-doubt or scrutiny, only the simple pursuit of curiosity, for its own sake. If the outcome is pleasing, that's a bonus – but it's not the point.

Being in this place gives me access to joy, a feeling that is both a reward and a guide. Because moments of joy give us clues: they tell us about what we like, what motivates us, what feels fulfilling. What keeps our Creative Ecosystem wheel turning.

In a world that has taught us to obsess over results and achievements, the act of creating purely for joy can feel like swimming against the current. But it's worth doing.

If you don't know where to start, try the exercise on the right. When you do, notice how the experience of joy ripples into other parts of your day.

<u>Jenny Bowers</u>
Illustrator & Art Director
UK

I love to make things, be it a piece of pottery, a set for a play, or growing flowers and vegetables. I am not an expert on any of these things but I just like having a go, using my hands, seeing how things are made and taking the opportunity to be taught things by people.

I don't mind if what I make isn't successful, that's not how I measure it. It feeds my Creative Ecosystem and reminds me to think and look and see beyond what I do for a job. It takes me away from familiar materials and processes which can become habitual and unsurprising.

For me, to keep being creative is to keep being surprised. Life is busy, as it is for everyone, but I try to squeeze things in that take me away from my daily routine.

I USED TO LOVE...

Unearth joy by revisiting activities you once loved.

List up to five of your favourite things to do when you were little, before you were 13 years old.

During these activities, you'd be so completely engaged that you lost track of time and awareness of yourself.

They could be anything - building with blocks, making up stories or playing an instrument.

How could you do a version of the same activity today, or this week?

Savour memories

As kids, tucked away in our grandparents' caravan, my cousin and I would play the same game over and over again. I would meticulously draw a typewriter keyboard on a piece of paper, the lettered keys neat and accurate. I, the secretary, would proceed to type, tapping my fingers vigorously on the paper. My cousin would sit across from me and watch – he was, of course, the boss.

This make-believe world we created is one of my fondest memories. Sadly it didn't come with a souvenir, but over the years I have made a point of holding onto small objects that transport me back to past happinesses – photographs, stones, a drawing. These everyday items can hold within them the fleeting details of an experience, and help us reconnect to how it felt.

Dr Sonja Lyubomirsky, a leading expert in positive psychology, has found that this kind of reconnection is worth doing. Her research shows that simply thinking about past happy experiences can boost life satisfaction – more so than writing or talking about these happy experiences.[46]

Our memories are a personal library of stories, songs and sensations that can connect us to joy in this moment, even if joy isn't present right now. Reflecting on them can also reveal details we thought we'd forgotten – textures, smells or fleeting emotions. These subtle, sensory memory fragments can even become a starting point for a new creative project.

Preserve the vibrancy of your experiences and let your inner library inspire you. This way, you can develop a sense of continuity between who you were, who you are and what you create.

Kangan Arora
Art Director, Illustrator & Designer
India/UK

After the short two weeks I get to travel home to India each year, I always leave creatively energised: soaking up all the colours, all the light, all the joy and bringing it back with me to last until my next visit. London provides plenty of inspiration too, but the yearning for home and family and what was once familiar outweighs it every time.

In the studio, I hold an archive of 20 years of photographs and ephemera... colour stories, architectural details, street wares, temples and food, people and festivals. These memories are the evocative details that often spark new ideas for a project.

HAPPY MEMORIES

1. Think of a happy memory – a time you felt connected, fulfilled, excited, or were simply having fun. Instead of writing it down, replay in your mind how it felt, in as much detail as possible. Let yourself enjoy that moment all over again.

2. Do this for eight minutes, three days a week – and notice how your overall satisfaction with life improves.

This exercise is inspired by Dr Sonja Lyubomirsky and her team.

Let go of perfection

Like so many of us, I often stop before I even start to create something. I've barely formed the idea before my mind puts on the brakes: someone else has done it better, it won't work, I don't know what the end result will look like. In my Creative Wellbeing Insights survey, 87% of respondents said they question if they are good enough. Some were young students, many had impressive careers stretching back 40+ years. No matter our experience, it's a difficult thought process to shake.

Last year, I was lucky enough to find myself on a white sandy beach on Australia's east coast. The Great Barrier Reef stretched for miles in each direction, and some of its brightly coloured corals had washed up on the shore. As I ambled along, adoring their strange shapes, I noticed that some of them reminded me of letters. I was compelled to create a whole set, and 'My A–Z guide for coral reef preservation' was born, together with my coral alphabet. I posted an image of my creation online, and it hit close to 800k views before the week was over. The comments poured in. Unfortunately, "this is the coolest thing I've ever seen in my life!" quickly became "wow, this is illegible, you need to study design more". I've censored the worst ones.

It didn't help that in my sunbaked state I'd overlooked the letter W, so the set was a letter short. But that didn't matter because I love our underwater forests, I'm passionate about preserving them, and I loved my day on the beach playing around with coral. Multiple people have been inspired to send me their versions of the alphabet, which brings me more joy – and some kindly sent just the letter W.

There was no need for my alphabet to be perfect, or even complete. Had I let my usual doubts put a stop to my creativity, I would never have made my coral alphabet at all. Rather than striving for perfection, we're far better taking a small step forward here and now.

And the best place to start is – you guessed it – with something that brings you joy.

Ji Lee
Designer
USA

I've made a life-long mission of always being in touch with the child in me: the ever curious, playful, nonsensical, mischievous at times, and always fun-loving kid. To see things like a child and to feel the freedom and the confidence to express myself is liberating but requires constant work.

I must remind myself of the importance of seeing the world with a curious mind and making things without overthinking, for the sake of making them and enjoying the process. This is worth every effort because in the moment of making things that I love, anxieties and insecurities disappear and I feel happy again.

SPACE FOR 'MISTAKES'

There are few things more freeing than making a mess. Pick a random object to sketch. Now draw it:

1. With your eyes closed.
2. With your non-dominant hand.

Get started

There's a trick I learned a few years ago that changed the way I work. It goes like this: set a timer for three minutes, and commit to either starting something, or taking a break. For the rest of those three minutes, do exactly that – start a creative task (like a sketch, a sentence, a list of ideas) or enjoy an intentional pause (you might stretch, make tea, look out of the window). The magic of the trick is that it locks you into the present moment. This short fragment of time – here, now – is all you need to think about. It's amazing the momentum that creates.

Every great achievement is made up of countless small tasks. A 500-page novel is made up of many shorter phrases and paragraphs; a client presentation comes together image by image, slide by slide. Doing something small, now, is enough. Which is to say: you are enough. On harder days the task might be as simple as doing the washing up, and that's OK.

Grounding into the present moment is a brilliant way to beat overwhelm, and also a wonderfully useful way to spend your time in a way that is true to you. As you look at the task in front of you, you might ask: does this bring me joy? An answer of 'yes' is a guiding light that can lead you onward. (As you uncover clues about yourself in this way, you may find it helpful to revisit the values and goals you uncovered in Chapter 1: Connection).

When we understand ourselves in this way, it becomes a lot easier to channel time and energy into activities that feel meaningful. This does more than help us achieve the things we want – research shows that engaging in work that aligns with your values is associated with higher wellbeing and lower levels of burnout.[47]

Julie Solvstrom
Illustrator & Lettering Artist
Canada/Denmark

I took it slow. Like, really slow. We're talking years. I'm risk-averse to a fault, and nothing about the idea of flipping my desk upside down and storming away from all sense of security was appealing to me.

So, I settled in for the long haul. I spent every spare moment doing the thing I deeply loved. In my case this was drawing letters. Every morning, every evening, every lunch break, and every holiday. I would go through sketchbooks like people go through underwear.

As my work got better, *I found my own voice and* style. I transitioned one small, cautious, step at a time, into the course I'm on now. It's the only one I ever want to be on.

THREE MINUTES!

A tiny time commitment is sometimes all you need to kickstart action.

1.
Pick a task that you can commit to working on for three minutes.

2.
Break it into the smallest possible action. For example, instead of “write the blog post”, start with “write one sentence about what the blog post is about”.

3.
Visualise how it will feel to complete this small action - relief, satisfaction, pride.

4.
Set a timer for three minutes, and get started.

(Sometimes just starting can build momentum - keep going if it carries you!)

How do you get into the flow?

Getting into the flow is a personal process: what works for me might not work for you. Some of us need structure, others spontaneity. Some need silence, others sound. It's a case of figuring out how to shape your surroundings, habits and mindset in a way that works for you.

The wide and wonderful range of answers creatives gave to the question "how do you get into the flow?" in my Creative Wellbeing Insights survey show just how true this is.[48]

Setting the scene

"I need to take care of basic things before being able to fully concentrate: eat if I'm hungry, have a nap if I'm tired, organise the space if it's messy and so on..."

"I find my flow happens in the evening, quiet late night working is a sweetspot for me, but it's hard to achieve in a world built for early birds."

"Breakfast is very important for me, it's a time for relaxing and centering. I sketch letters in a notebook also... they don't need to be related to the projects I'm working on, but they help me put my eyes and brain in motion!"

"Tidying and removing distractions."

"Breathing techniques, playing guitar."

"Clear my desk, arrange books."

"Getting amongst my products, working directly with them."

"Make a cup of coffee."

"Shower, to-do lists, just focus."

"I usually listen to something, or body-doubling really helps."

"Check my plants."

"Pull all the materials out."

Sound on/off

"Put on classical music, prioritise creativity over mundane tasks."

"I make sure there's silence or that I have blocked out sound. And I put my phone on do not disturb."

"Be surrounded by people who are working as well, and white noise."

"I start with a cup of latte, some music or a podcast as a background, it depends on the project. I light an incense to move the energy too."

"I keep my work space clean and clear, and always tunes, tunes, tunes."

"Quietness, no distractions."

Replacing thought with action

"Just start doing it. Don't think."

"By doing."

"Start with the easiest task in my to do list and whack it out so I can immediately cross it off my list."

WHAT HELPS YOU GET IN THE ZONE?

ELIZABETH OLWEN
Print & Pattern Designer

THE JOY OF CREATIVE LIFE

Just thinking about Elizabeth makes me smile! Her sunny personality beams through her colourful floral and geometric designs. She is a Canadian designer living in Portugal, who creates with the intention of spreading beauty and amplifying joy.

What activities bring you joy and how do they influence your work?
Initially I thought my creativity would be on tap – on full blast for a while, and then I'd turn it off. Realising how much creativity is in my everyday life, it opened me to new things. I've always loved fashion, for example. So now I give myself extra time to get dressed – every outfit is a composition, a creative expression. I'm pairing colours and shapes and textures. It's a design activity for myself, and it brings me joy!

Taking a pause is also extremely essential because if I'm taking a break to dance, even if it's just me at home with headphones, that's a creative act for me. Although I've gotten rid of a lot of guilt, it's still hard not to feel it at times. But I'm far more empowered when I gift myself the joy of beautiful experience.

How have you navigated and overcome creative resistance?
I used to constantly think "I should have a daily practice". Then I started working with a creative coach and discovered I needed deeper purpose and meaning in my work. She helped me see that when I followed my own path – doing things my way, not the industry's – it was always successful and rewarding. It gave me a lot of confidence to create my own path.

As a solo creative, how do you find joy in collaboration?
I find joy in the retreats and workshops I organise. I create spaces where creativity becomes an act of self-love and expression, not focused on the outcome. It's about enjoying the process and connecting with others. My agent is also a great collaborator and we bounce ideas off each other. Having always worked solo, it's wonderful to have someone catch my ideas and throw them back with a new perspective.

How do you get into flow state?
I always keep my notebook with me, constantly writing, drawing, and capturing my ideas. By the time I need to sit down and work, I've already done my future self a favour by engaging with my creativity on such a consistent basis. I just return to my sketchbook where I have a million ideas. I often feel like a vessel for the things I'm exploring in life. I let creativity flow through me along with everything I'm learning. My passions, how I feel about the world, life and joy.

1

2

3

4

5

6

7

1-3 Elizabeth's moodboards, sketches and work in progress

4 Cosmic Floral

5 Shape of Love

6-7 Elizabeth's products, photos by Eglė Duleckytė

Share joy

There were a few years, earlier in my career, when I shared a studio space in Shoreditch, London, with a group of illustrators and animators called Peepshow Collective. We were tucked away in a chaotic space filled with human-sized pencils and paint tins and miniature paper-cut hands and heads.

During that time, I looked forward to work every morning. We'd get together for lunch every day, laugh at the absurdities that came with our jobs, and dream up projects to collaborate on. No matter what problems the day would bring, I knew we'd find a way to see the funny side. It was messy, magical, and the perfect blend of camaraderie and creativity.

More often than not, sharing our days with others makes everything a bit more cheerful. Research shows that our experiences intensify when shared, making good times feel even more special.[49]

When our experiences are more vivid, we tend to notice more about them – about ourselves, our emotions, our surroundings. These details can prompt new ideas, or show us patterns and stories to build on. In this way, sharing moments with others is a kind of creative fuel – one that can connect our creativity more closely to the nuance and truth of our experiences.

Jess Goldsmith
Illustrator & Lettering Artist
Women of Type
USA

Joy isn't just personal in the Women of Type community. It uplifts everyone and makes our creative work even more impactful. When my peers share their joy and encouragement about my work, it helps me take risks, try new things, and grow in ways I may not have otherwise.

I want to continue building a space where we share that joy, evolve together, refine our craft, and create with a deeper purpose. Creativity thrives in connection, inspiration, fun, and joy. I'm grateful to be able to be both a part of and a facilitator of this with Women of Type.

ELEMENTS
Visualisation Exercise

FIRE

Find a space where you can sit comfortably, alone or with a group of friends. If you're alone, imagine you're part of a circle of people you feel connected to. Close your eyes, take a deep breath and picture a warm, glowing fire at the centre of your circle.

Feel the fire's warmth radiating outward, wrapping you in a comforting embrace. Let this sensation fill your body.

Picture everyone around the fire holding a glowing ember that represents their own joy. Take turns (in reality or in your imagination) sharing a word that makes you happy, like 'adventure', 'yellow', or 'summer'. Each word becomes a spark, feeding the fire and making it brighter.

Extend your arms toward the fire, palms open. Imagine holding the fire's warmth and energy in your hands. Slowly lift your arms, then move them outward, as if spreading this light and joy to those around you.

As the fire settles, imagine it leaving behind an ember that glows with connection and energy. Pick it up, hold onto this warmth and carry it forward into the rest of your day.

Play together

A few years ago, I met up with a creative friend – Jonna Saarinen, a textile designer – at a London museum. Rather than meet for coffee, we made a different plan. We each brought along a set of pastels and a notebook, and sat together to sketch the museum's summer herb garden. Hours melted by as we coloured our pages, talked about life, and shared our frustrations at work.

Something wonderful happened as the afternoon went by: it was as though we were colouring our stresses away, leaving us lighter with each stroke. The outcome of our drawings was far from professional, but our anxieties had lifted. The effect was so profound, we committed to making it a regular activity – we called it KraftKlub. We have since taken our pencils to the Barbican, watercolours to Kew Gardens, and felt tip pens to Dulwich Picture Gallery. Every time, we've left feeling lighter, more uplifted.

When the pandemic hit, we carried on. We ordered playdough and chose vegetables from our fridge to sculpt. We picked photos of a building we had both visited in Finland and collaged away.

The idea was so simple, and so fun, that we had to share it. We put out an open invitation through our social networks, and 20 people joined us on a virtual retro summer holiday to Finland, where we 'took a coach trip' back to the 1970s. We visited (virtually) the Tampella textile factory, the Arabia pottery studios, and artist workshops before collaging our own patterns to adorn fabric or a coffee pot.

Virtual crafting trips like this became a regular public online event throughout the lockdowns. We found a way to play together, even when the world was keeping us apart. Could you create your own version of the KraftKlub?

Jonna Saarinen
Textile Designer &
KraftKlub Co-Founder
Finland

If you don't have the time and space to think, it's really hard to try to be creative on top of that. In London, life is sometimes so busy you don't even notice February has turned into May.

Therefore, it's even more vital to create something for fun, where the end result doesn't matter. If you are under financial and time pressure, all of that will evaporate.

CREATE YOUR OWN KRAFTKLUB

1.
Invite a friend (or a few) and gather some creative tools to work with: paper, pencils, clay, paints, or anything you feel inspired to use.

2.
Ask everyone to think of a happy memory. Identify a specific detail or object from that memory that stands out, like a teapot, a flower, a favourite pet dog.

3.
Using your chosen tools, create something inspired by the detail you picked.

For example:
Collage a teapot.
Draw a flower.
Sculpt a dog.

4.
As you work, take turns sharing the story behind your happy memory. Talk about what made it meaningful, how it felt, and why you chose the detail you're crafting.

JONATHAN KENYON

Co-Founder & Executive Creative Director

FROM STREET ART TO GLOBAL AGENCY

More than anyone I personally know of, co-founders Jonathan Kenyon and John Glasgow have kept making at the core of their practice – since their beginnings as a South London street art collective through to their work today heading up global brand design agency Vault49 in New York City. They share a passion for evoking joy through public art, and it truly shows in the energetic output of their commercial work.

Making has always been central to your practice. How has that hands-on ethos evolved as Vault49 has grown, and do you think it remains vital?

Vault49 emerged from the cultural margins as a street art collective. We exist because of a deep and meaningful connection to culture and community.

Today, we're a brand design and innovation agency, and being 'hands-on' is more important than ever. We connect brands to people through human stories, and a crafted approach to design can be a large part of authentic storytelling. When we exist in a world of emotionless click-button content, the counterpoint to that is craft. The hands that tell the story can often be the story.

Vault49 is known for its playful approach to design. How do you keep that sense of play alive across your team and projects?

It's cultural. Play is infectious. Both John and I identify with playfulness. We find it to be the most attractive character trait. When we show up in the studio playfully, others respond, and the same is true in reverse. Our team frequently presents their passions inside and outside of design to the whole team, and the vulnerability of that process deepens friendships and opens up a greater sense of play.

Do you have a personal ritual or process for reconnecting with making when you feel creatively drained?

Art, to me, is taking what is within myself and putting it on the outside to be seen. When I have lost connection to one aspect of my creativity, I focus on bringing movement to my whole. My ritual is dance. It fills my energetic body with momentum and eventually, inevitably, breaks through any blocked aspect of my creative expression.

Collaboration is at the heart of your work. How do you create an environment where diverse ideas and perspectives can thrive?

Humility alongside healthy egos. We encourage our team to be confident in their expertise and have the ego to stand up for their ideas and convictions. But equally to have the humility to accept that everyone has their unique talents and to both allow space and provide support for the abilities of their colleagues.

1

2

3

4-5

6

1-2 Black Lives Matter Screenprinted posters

3 Lay's Kitchen Potato printing pop-up experience

4-6 Big Easy Kombucha Packaging Process and final design

Harvest gratitude

Every morning, I start my day with my pen in my hand. I write a page, freeflow, whatever comes to mind – a journalling practice I learned from *The Artist's Way*. It's come to be a brilliant way to listen to myself, before the day runs away with me. I always end the page writing down what I'm grateful for, followed by what I want to focus on that day.

Gratitude can simply be an internal thought – "I am thankful". It can also be a gift you give to others with words and actions that say "thank you, I appreciate you". Studies show that feeling gratitude and performing acts of gratitude improve life satisfaction and reduce symptoms of anxiety and depression.[50] Gratitude can even increase feelings of joy, which in turn prompts feelings of gratitude. How's that for a happy upward spiral![51]

When we feel thankful for what we have, we're more likely to approach challenges with a sense of possibility, rather than focusing on what is lacking. It takes effort, but it's worth it.

So, try making 'harvesting gratitude' a regular practice. If every day feels like too much, pause monthly or seasonally to notice and appreciate the good in life.

When I reflect on what I'm thankful for, I can't help but see the richness around me – a feeling of abundance that I can then channel into my creative pursuits. And showing our gratitude to others brings them closer to us. This noticing, giving and receiving, is a way of creating something bigger than ourselves, together.

Radim Malinic
Designer & Author
Brand Nu
Czech Republic/UK

I am grateful for morning inspiration that brings ideas that refuse to be ignored, while blank pages offer freedom to express my soul. Unfinished drafts are simply evolving stories; moments of doubt hide breakthroughs waiting to emerge.

Long-drawn commissions teach me endurance; constant revisions remind me great things take time. Harsh criticism reveals more about others than myself. Creative outlets help me heal during stress, and working in isolation connects me with my vision.

Financial uncertainty is the price of freedom from soul-crushing alternatives. When I celebrate my uniqueness, it leads to my self-acceptance. I cherish creative connections, reminding me I'm not alone in how I feel.

Physical and mental exhaustion proves I'm bringing something into existence. Though creativity can be super hard, it reminds me I'm alive!

GRATITUDE RIPPLE

Commit to a daily practice of
writing down or saying out loud
three things you're grateful for:
- about yourself
- about someone else
- about the world around you.

Plant future seeds

An important, but uncomfortable, part of the Creation stage is getting feedback – sometimes when you don't ask for it. It can be challenging to hear, but it's also an important opportunity.

As we reach the end of this journey together, I invite you to give yourself some thoughtful feedback. Together, we've made our way through five chapters, five steps in the creative process, and all kinds of exercises that have, I hope, brought new ways of thinking off the page and into your everyday life. Before you close this book, I invite you to think back on what you've learned and let it guide your next steps.

Do this by writing a letter to your future self. You may remember my description of doing just this at the beginning of Chapter 1: Connection – how the written dialogues between past and future versions of my changing self have anchored me as I've grown. I hope for the same for you. Think of your letter as a conversation across time, a way to hold onto the insights you've had and commitments you've made while reading this book.

Ask yourself:

What have you learned about your creativity and wellbeing?
What ideas have resonated with you?
What actions will you commit to moving forward?
What encouragement do you want to give your future self?

You can also include questions for your future self, like: What makes you happy? Are you still spending time with a new creative hobby? How's your energy, and where are you finding more of it? Don't forget to date your letter, so you can join the dots through time.

In many ways – and especially through letter writing – exploring the Joy input of the Creative Ecosystem wheel links us right back to where we started, with Connection. We have come full circle, energised by what feels good and guided by what matters.

CREATIVE ECOSYSTEM

WRITE A LETTER TO YOUR FUTURE SELF

Set a reminder to read your letter in six months or a year - whatever feels right. Repeat this exercise, to reach ahead to yet another future you, and keep the chain of reflection going.

Closing the circle

Writing this book has, once again, shown me the dualities in life. The very ideas I explored and championed – how to fuel creativity, protect wellbeing and stay inspired – were tested hard in the process of getting them on the page.

Thankfully, the Creative Ecosystem model did its job. The Connection input helped me build the book around what really matters to me – my connection with nature and my belief in the power of positive creativity to bring people together. The Wonder input helped me to step back and explore fields far beyond design, from positive psychology and behavioural science to mindfulness. And, even as I pored over research on the power of creative rest, the Pause input was a reminder to look up from my screen and go for walks, to live what I was writing.

Surprisingly, the most beautiful part of articulating the Creative Ecosystem model has been discovering new layers of it. I wasn't just advocating for creative wellbeing, I was experiencing it in new ways. Giving myself time away from the book, conquering the comparisons to other creative authors out there, and trusting the process became as much a part of this journey as the words themselves. The ideas and landscape were familiar, but I found new kinds of clarity and meaning in them.

And now, on this last page, I find myself grateful. Not only for this journey, but for you, the reader, coming along with me. I hope this book has sparked something for you, as writing it has for me. May your own Creative Ecosystem sustain and inspire you, wherever your path leads.

Check-in

REFLECT ON YOUR INPUTS

Consider the five input areas in your life:

CONNECTION for purpose
WONDER for inspiration
PAUSE for intuition
MOVEMENT for resilience
JOY for energy

How good do you feel in each area right now. Rate your inputs from 1 (needs attention) to 5 (feeling great!) by colouring the wheel in.

You'll clearly see which parts of your Creative Ecosystem need more attention. Revisit that chapter, and explore the exercises there to find the creative fuel you need. Come back to this page in six months time. Has your score changed?

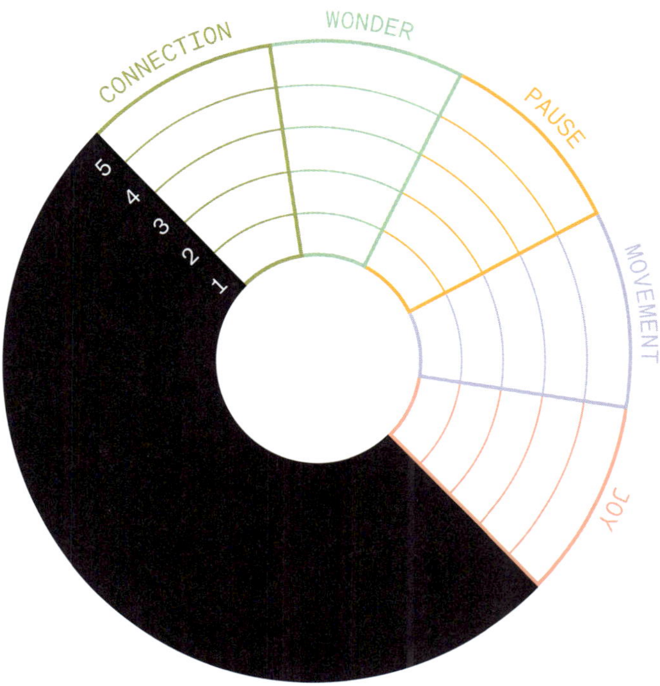

The Creative Ecosystem at a glance

To sustain your creative wellbeing, balance your creative outputs with your nourishing inputs.

Five core inputs:

Connection

Connect who you are with what you do to nurture your **purpose.**

Wonder

Explore the ordinary with curiosity to nurture your **inspiration.**

...supported by creative process thinking:

Briefing

Think of it like the *Briefing stage*, and it will help you to focus on your values, which will bring you meaning.

Research

See it like the *Research stage*, and it will help you open your mind and find the unusual in the usual.

© Studio Emmi
CreativeEcosystem.org

CREATIVE ECOSYSTEM

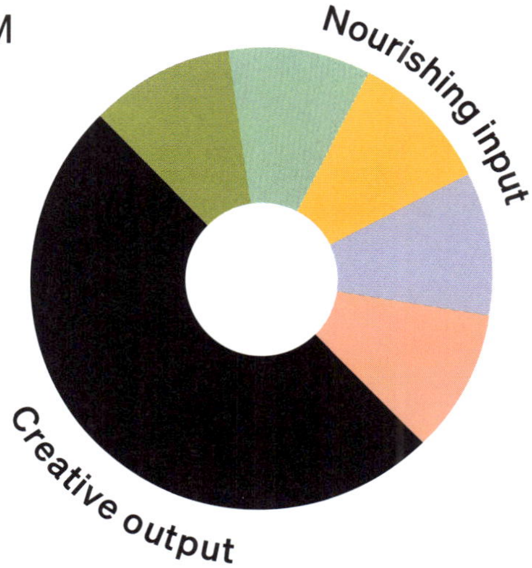

Pause	Movement	Joy
Book in time for solitude and reflection to nurture your **intuition.**	Stay fluid and evolve with the process to nurture your **resilience.**	Enjoy immersing yourself in an activity to nurture your **energy**.

Ideation	Development	Creation
Consider it like the *Ideation stage*, and it will guide your creative spirit.	Frame it like the *Development stage*, and and it will help your mind and body stay flexible.	Treat it like the *Creation stage*, and it will help you find your spark.

Thank you

To everyone I met on my travels, near and far – thank you. Your openness in sharing what keeps you going and what holds you back helped shape the thinking behind the Creative Ecosystem model.

I'm especially grateful to the 100+ creatives from 26 countries who so generously gave their time and contributed to this book through the *Wellbeing Insights Report*, in-depth interviews, and by sharing their reflections as quotes. Thank you for your generosity, wisdom and trust.

Thank you to my Editor, Becca Warner, for helping me find the right words (and gently nudging the wrong ones out of the way), for your care, skill and belief in this book.

And to every single one of you who encouraged me along the way. From the strangers who asked me to write a book after my talk, to friends and colleagues who shared thoughtful, honest feedback, to my loved ones who live this creative journey with me each day.

This book came to life through all of you.

With love,
Emmi

MY GREAT BARRIER REEF CORAL ALPHABET
A thank you to you all, from A to Z – including those whose names begin with W.

References

1
Never Not Creative. (2024). *Mentally-Healthy 2024*: The results. Never Not Creative.
https://www.nevernotcreative.org/mentally-healthy-2024-survey

2
Gallup. (2020). *Gallup's Perspective on Employee Burnout: Causes and Cures.* Gallup, Inc.
https://www.gallup.com/workplace/282668/employee-burnout-perspective-paper.aspx

3
Gallup. (2024). *State of the Global Workplace: 2024 Report*. Gallup, Inc.
https://www.gallup.com/workplace/349484/state-of-the-global-workplace.aspx

4
Shorter, G. W., McCann, S., & McIlherron, L. (2018). *Changing Arts and Minds: A survey of health and wellbeing in the creative sector.* Ulster University.
https://pure.ulster.ac.uk/en/publications/c0c88b15-7368-42d2-aaa2-1adf51520261

5, 6
Salonen, E. (2023). *Creative Wellbeing Insights: How creative minds manage stress and thrive in the creative industry.* Studio Emmi.
https://www.creativeecosystem.org/resources

7
PwC. (2023). *PwC's 2023 Employee Financial Wellness Survey.* PwC.
https://pwc.com/us/en/services/consulting/business-transformation/library/employee-financial-wellness-survey.html

8
TIAA Institute. (2024). *Connecting Mental and Financial Wellbeing: Insights for Employers.* TIAA.
https://www.tiaa.org/public/institute/publication/2024/connecting-mental-and-financial-wellbeing

9
Lu, J. G., Hafenbrack, A. C., Eastwick, P. W., Wang, D. J., Maddux, W. W., & Galinsky, A. D. (2017). "Going out" of the box: Close intercultural friendships and romantic relationships spark creativity, workplace innovation, and entrepreneurship. *Journal of Applied Psychology, 102*(7), 1091–1108.
https://doi.org/10.1037/apl0000212

10
Ascigil, E., Gunaydin, G., Selcuk, E., Sandstrom, G., & Aydin, E. (2023). Minimal social interactions and life satisfaction: The role of greeting, thanking, and conversing. *Social Psychological and Personality Science, 16*(2), 268–278.
https://doi.org/10.1177/19485506231209793

11
Mongrain, M., Chin, J. M., & Shapira, L. B. (2011). Practicing compassion increases happiness and self-esteem. *Journal of Happiness Studies, 12*(6), 963–981. https://doi.org/10.1007/s10902-010-9239-1

12
Haugan G, Eriksson M, editors. *Health Promotion in Health Care – Vital Theories and Research* [Internet]. Cham (CH): Springer; 2021. PMID: 36315659. https://www.ncbi.nlm.nih.gov/books/NBK585660

13
Mann, S., & Cadman, R. (2014). Does Being Bored Make Us More Creative? *Creativity Research Journal, 26*(2), 165–173. https://doi.org/10.1080/10400419.2014.901073

14
Keltner, D., & Haidt, J. (2003). Approaching awe, a moral, spiritual, and aesthetic emotion. *Cognition and Emotion, 17*(2), 297–314. https://doi.org/10.1080/02699930302297

15
Rudd, M., Aaker, J., & Vohs, K. D. (2012). Awe expands people's perception of time, alters decision making, and enhances well-being. *Psychological Science, 23*(10), 1130–1136. https://doi.org/10.1177/0956797612438731

16
Salonen. (2023). *Creative Wellbeing Insights.* Studio Emmi.

17
Nadile, E. M., Alfonso, E., Barreiros, B. M., Bevan-Thomas, W. D., Brownell, S. E., Chin, M. R., Ferreira, I., Ford, S. A., Gin, L. E., Gomez-Rosado, J. O., Gooding, G., Heiden, A., Hutt, A. E., King, M. L., Perez, S. G., Rivera Camacho, Y. I., Salcedo, F., Sellas, C. F., Sinda, K. A., Stahlhut, K. N., Stephens, M. D., Wiesenthal, N. J., Williams, K. D., Zheng, Y., & Cooper, K. M. (2021). Call on me! Undergraduates' perceptions of voluntarily asking and answering questions in front of large-enrollment science classes. *PLOS ONE, 16*(1), e0243731. https://doi.org/10.1371/journal.pone.0243731

18
Hargadon, A. B., & Bechky, B. A. (2006). When Collections of Creatives Become Creative Collectives: A Field Study of Problem Solving at Work. *Organization Science, 17*(4), 484–500. https://doi.org/10.1287/orsc.1060.0200

19
Irving, Z. C., McGrath, C., Flynn, L., Glasser, A., & Mills, C. (2024). The shower effect: Mind wandering facilitates creative incubation during moderately engaging activities. *Psychology of Aesthetics, Creativity, and the Arts, 18*(6), 1096–1107. https://doi.org/10.1037/aca0000516

20
Raffaelli, Q., Malusa, R., de Stefano, N-A., Andrews, E., Grilli, M. D., Mills, C., Zabelina, D. L., & Andrews-Hanna, J. R. (2024). Creative Minds at Rest: Creative Individuals are More Associative and Engaged with Their Idle Thoughts. *Creativity Research Journal, 36*(3), 396–412.
https://doi.org/10.1080/10400419.2023.2227477

21
Albulescu, P., Macsinga, I., Rusu, A., Sulea, C., Bodnaru, A., & Tulbure, B. T. (2022). "Give me a break!" A systematic review and meta-analysis on the efficacy of micro-breaks for increasing well-being and performance. *PLOS ONE, 17*(8), e0272460.
https://doi.org/10.1371/journal.pone.0272460

22
Giurge, L. M., Whillans, A. V., & West, C. (2020). Why time poverty matters for individuals, organisations and nations. *Nature Human Behaviour*, *4*(10), 993–1003.
https://doi.org/10.1038/s41562-020-0920-z

23
Whillans, A. (2019). Time for Happiness. *Harvard Business Review*.
https://hbr.org/2019/01/time-for-happiness

24
Münzel, T., Gori, T., Babisch, W., & Basner, M. (2014). Cardiovascular effects of environmental noise exposure. *European Heart Journal, 35*(13), 829–836.
https://doi.org/10.1093/eurheartj/ehu030

25
Mertens, S., Herberz, M., Hahnel, U. J. J., & Brosch, T. (2022). The effectiveness of nudging: A meta-analysis of choice architecture interventions across behavioral domains. *Proceedings of the National Academy of Sciences, 119*(1), e2107346118.
https://doi.org/10.1073/pnas.2107346118

26
Salonen. (2023). *Creative Wellbeing Insights.* Studio Emmi.

27
Voutilainen, O., Korhonen, K., Ovaska, U., & Vihinen, H. (2021). *Mökkibarometri 2021.* Luonnonvarakeskus (Luke).
https://urn.fi/URN:ISBN:978-952-380-237-7

28
Statistics Finland. (2022). *Vital statistics and population, 2021* [Data set]. StatFin.
https://pxdata.stat.fi/PxWeb/pxweb/en/StatFin/StatFin__synt/statfin_synt_pxt_12dx.px

29
van den Berg, M. M. H. E., Maas, J., Muller, R., Braun, A., Kaandorp, W., van Lien, R., van Poppel, M. N. M., van Mechelen, W., & van den Berg, A. E. (2015). Autonomic Nervous System Responses to Viewing Green and Built Settings: Differentiating Between Sympathetic and Parasympathetic Activity. *International Journal of Environmental Research and Public Health, 12*(12), 15860–15874. https://doi.org/10.3390/ijerph121215026

30
Owens, M., & Bunce, H. (2023). The effect of brief exposure to virtual nature on mental wellbeing in adolescents. *Scientific Reports, 13*, 17769. https://doi.org/10.1038/s41598-023-44717-z

31
Hogan, M. J. (2005). Zautra's Terror: Thinking about emotions, stress, and health. *The Irish Psychologist, 32*(1), 1–8. https://michaelhoganpsychology.com/wp-content/uploads/2015/08/zautras-terror.pdf

32
Silva, L. R. B., Seguro, C. S., de Oliveira, C. G. A., Santos, P. O. S., de Oliveira, J. C. M., de Souza Filho, L. F. M., de Paula Júnior, C. A., Gentil, P., & Rebelo, A. C. S. (2020). Physical Inactivity is Associated With Increased Levels of Anxiety, Depression, and Stress in Brazilians During the COVID-19 Pandemic: A Cross-Sectional Study. *Frontiers in Psychiatry, 11,* Article 565291. https://doi.org/10.3389/fpsyt.2020.565291

33
World Health Organization. (n.d.). Physical activity. Retrieved February 14, 2025, from https://who.int/news-room/fact-sheets/detail/physical-activity

34
Wilson, T. D., & Gilbert, D. T. (2003). Affective Forecasting. *Advances in Experimental Social Psychology, 35*, 345–411. https://doi.org/10.1016/S0065-2601(03)01006-2

35
Baumeister, R. F., Bratslavsky, E., Finkenauer, C., & Vohs, K. D. (2001). Bad is Stronger than Good. *Review of General Psychology, 5*(4), 323–370. https://doi.org/10.1037/1089-2680.5.4.323

36
Salonen. (2023). *Creative Wellbeing Insights.* Studio Emmi.

37, 38
Lyubomirsky, S., Sheldon, K. M., & Schkade, D. (2005). Pursuing Happiness: The Architecture of Sustainable Change *Review of General Psychology, 9*(2), 111–131. https://doi.org/10.1037/1089-2680.9.2.111

39
Kuiper, N. A. (2012). Humor and resiliency: Resiliency: Towards a Process Model of Coping and Growth. *Europe's Journal of Psychology, 8*(3), 475–491. https://doi.org/10.5964/ejop.v8i3.464

40
Ligeza, T. S., Maciejczyk, M., Wyczesany, M., & Junghöfer, M. (2022). The effects of a single aerobic exercise session on mood and neural emotional reactivity in depressed and healthy young adults: A late positive potential study. *Psychophysiology, 60*(e14137). https://doi.org/10.1111/psyp.14137

41
Oppezzo, M., & Schwartz, D. L. (2014). Give your ideas some legs: The positive effect of walking on creative thinking. *Journal of Experimental Psychology: Learning, Memory, and Cognition, 40*(4), 1142–1152. https://doi.org/10.1037/a0036577

42
National Health Service. (n.d.). Exercise: Health benefits. NHS. Retrieved March 8, 2025, from https://nhs.uk/live-well/exercise/exercise-health-benefits

43
Chapman, B. P., Fiscella, K., Kawachi, I., Duberstein, P., & Muennig, P. (2013). Emotion suppression and mortality risk over a 12-year follow-up. *Journal of Psychosomatic Research, 75*(4), 381–385. https://doi.org/10.1016/j.jpsychores.2013.07.014

44
Trivedi, G., Sharma, K., Saboo, B., Kathirvel, S., Konat, A., Zapadia, V., Prajapati, P. J., Benani, U., Patel, K., & Shah, S. (2023). Humming (Simple Bhramari Pranayama) as a Stress Buster: A Holter-Based Study to Analyze Heart Rate Variability (HRV) Parameters During Bhramari, Physical Activity, Emotional Stress, and Sleep. *Cureus, 15*(4), e37527. https://doi.org/10.7759/cureus.37527

45
Oppezzo & Schwartz. (2014). Give your ideas some legs: The positive effect of walking on creative thinking. *Journal of Experimental Psychology: Learning, Memory, and Cognition.*

46
Lyubomirsky, S., Sousa, L., & Dickerhoof, R. M. (2006). The costs and benefits of writing, talking, and thinking about life's triumphs and defeats. *Journal of Personality and Social Psychology, 90*(4), 692–708. https://doi.org/10.1037/0022-3514.90.4.692

47
Veage, S., Ciarrochi, J., Deane, F. P., Andresen, R., Oades, L. G., & Crowe, T. P. (2014). Value congruence, importance and success in the workplace: Links with well-being and burnout amongst mental health practitioners. *Journal of Contextual Behavioral Science, 3*(4), 258–264. https://doi.org/10.1016/j.jcbs.2014.06.004

48
Salonen. (2023). *Creative Wellbeing Insights.* Studio Emmi.

49
Boothby, E. J., Clark, M. S., & Bargh, J. A. (2014). Shared Experiences Are Amplified. *Psychological Science, 25*(12), 2209–2216. https://doi.org/10.1177/0956797614551162

50
Diniz, G., Korkes, L., Tristão, L. S., Pelegrini, R., Bellodi, P. L., & Bernardo, W. M. (2023). The effects of gratitude interventions: a systematic review and meta-analysis. *einstein (São Paulo), 21,* eRW0371. https://doi.org/10.31744/einstein_journal/2023RW0371

51
Watkins, P. C., Emmons, R. A., Greaves, M. R., & Bell, J. (2017). Joy is a distinct positive emotion: Assessment of joy and relationship to gratitude and well-being. *The Journal of Positive Psychology, 13*(5), 522–539.
https://doi.org/10.1080/17439760.2017.1414298